E G L I

## Date Due

| NOV 5 1980 | | |
|---|---|---|
| NOV 9 1982 | | |
| | | |
| | | |
| | | |
| | | |
| | | |
| | | |
| | | |
| | | |
| | | |
| | | |
| | | |
| | | |
| | | |
| | | |
| | | |
| | | |
| | | |
| | | |

DEMCO NO. 38-298

ESSAYS ON RECENT SOUTHERN POLITICS

# THE WALTER PRESCOTT WEBB MEMORIAL LECTURES: IV

THE WALTER PRESCOTT WEBB MEMORIAL LECTURES

# ESSAYS ON RECENT SOUTHERN POLITICS

BY

E. C. BARKSDALE

GEORGE NORRIS GREEN

T. HARRY WILLIAMS

*Introduction by John B. Connally*

*Edited by*
*Harold M. Hollingsworth*

PUBLISHED FOR THE UNIVERSITY OF TEXAS AT ARLINGTON
BY THE UNIVERSITY OF TEXAS PRESS, AUSTIN & LONDON

International Standard Book Number 0-292-70045-8
Library of Congress Catalog Card Number 79-115418
Copyright © 1970 by The University of Texas at Arlington
All Rights Reserved
Manufactured in the United States of America

# PREFACE

The fourth annual Walter Prescott Webb Memorial Lectures were held in Texas Hall of The University of Texas at Arlington on April 10, 1969. George Green and E. C. Barksdale, members of the history faculty at Arlington, presented the morning papers; the series concluded with an evening address by T. Harry Williams, Boyd Professor of History at Louisiana State University.

These lectures seek to memorialize a great historian by encouraging scholars, young and old, famous and obscure, to present the results of their research in a form that interests and inspires laymen and undergraduates as well as informs the scholarly community. The success of this venture is demonstrated by the favorable notices these volumes have received in the professional press and by the burgeoning attendance that required the sessions to be moved from a hall that holds 750 persons to one that accommodates over 3,000.

The continuation of this series has been insured by a generous gift from Mr. and Mrs. C. B. Smith, Sr., of Austin, and, if the Walter Prescott Webb Great Frontier Foundation Association achieves its goals, these lectures will be able to develop from a firm financial base.

Obviously W. P. Webb is not dead. His personality moti-
vates friends who knew and loved him; his ideas live in books
and articles; and his spirit of critical inquiry is manifest in
these essays.

HAROLD M. HOLLINGSWORTH

# CONTENTS

# INTRODUCTION

It is appropriate that this fourth series of Walter Prescott Webb Memorial Lectures deals with the contemporary South. Although Walter Webb was a historian, he was always as concerned with the present as with the past. He was perhaps even more concerned with the future. Neither he nor his books looked backward.

Webb was a Southerner. But he wasted no tears on lost causes. Instead, he addressed his fertile mind to finding solutions for the problems that plagued his section. In the 1930's he wrote *Divided We Stand*, which graphically documents the struggle of an emerging industrial South and West against an already industrialized North. In the 1950's he translated the bureaucratic prose of a government report into the clarion call, *More Water for Texas*. Neither Texas nor the South is as it was when he wrote. Much of this transformation may be credited to men like Webb, who saw what needed to be done and did it.

This brings to mind the thesis of the first essay in this volume. Dr. E. C. Barksdale, chairman of the History Department of The University of Texas at Arlington, suggests that this group of "doers"—the "power structure"—have generally taken a moderate stand in the gubernatorial battles of the last decade. Conservatism may have triumphed at the polls, but the substantial leadership has, more often than not, cast its vote for the more progressive candidate. Even the Deep South is changing, and, as Professor Barksdale demonstrates, the men who are leading the economic transformation of the South are also using their political influence to help close the political gap that still separates the South from much of the rest of the nation.

Texas, more than any other state in the old Confederacy, has profited from the dynamic enterprise of aggressive leaders who have transformed a land of cotton, cattle, and oil into a diversified industrial state. These leaders in oil, banking, construction, insurance, electronics, aeronautics, and agriculture have not insulated themselves from politics. While transforming the state economically, they have taken the time and effort to shape the political policies of Texas into the flexible, progressive form that characterizes the business enterprise of the state.

During the last decade these men have led in expanding and coordinating the system of higher education. They have supported efforts by the state to increase tourism and to preserve the rich heritage of natural beauty and wildlife. They have sought to implement a long-range water plan that would provide more water for Texas, not only in the immediate future, but also for decades to come. I am proud to have had a part in this task. I regret that we have not gone farther with

the water plan, constitutional revision, and a general moderni-
zation of our state government. But we could not have gone
as far as we did without the support of the substantial leadership in Texas.

This progressive spirit is not the only current in the Texas
political stream. East Texas is culturally and economically
linked with the old South; West Texas is emphatically the
West; South Texas owes a cultural debt to Mexico on its
western flank and an economic debt to the petrochemical and
aerospace industries on the eastern side. Texas is diverse. Its
politics is a politics of diversity. Texas is undergoing major
change and its political institutions reflect tensions that accom-
pany the change.

Dr. George Green's essay highlights one response to this
diverse society's struggle with rapid change. It is not easy to
watch long-cherished beliefs challenged by men whose motives
may be suspect, whose veracity may be in doubt. Change is
never easy. But despite the excesses of a few, the main current of Texas politics has not been right or left, but a reasoned
moderation, a progressive conservatism that has put its faith
in the future while preserving what is best from a diverse
heritage.

It is significant that Texas has produced far more than its
share of national leaders during the past generation. In con-
trast with Professor T. Harry Williams' description of Huey
P. Long, the style of such men as Sam Rayburn and Lyndon
Johnson was marked by compromise, the ability to find the

program that would do the greatest good for the greatest number while doing the least harm to settled successful institutions. These men possessed the ability and the will to plan for tomorrow without destroying what was best about today.

This approach is a natural product of the diversity that is the hallmark of Texas geography and culture. Those who seek and hold public office in Texas are, of necessity, schooled in a politics of diversity, an education that has served them as well in Washington as in Austin.

This brings my thoughts back to Walter Prescott Webb. I did not take his class when I was a student at The University of Texas at Austin. I knew him only as a figure striding across the campus. But I did not escape his influence. He was a Texas phenomenon with a reputation larger than life. Even from a distance it was obvious that his eminence was not a product of denying his roots, of adopting the values of an alien culture. Rather he was honored for understanding himself in relation to his own environment. By knowing himself and his land he was able to tell all of us something significant about ourselves. Therefore, as I turned my attention to the most pressing problems confronting Texas in the 1960's, it was no surprise to me when I often found that Walter Webb had been there before me. We honor ourselves in honoring this great Texan.

JOHN B. CONNALLY

ESSAYS ON RECENT SOUTHERN POLITICS

# The Power Structure and Southern
# Gubernatorial Conservatism

E. C. BARKSDALE

"THE POWER STRUCTURE and Southern Gubernatorial Conservatism" might more appropriately be titled "A Study in Perplexity, or Difficulties Encountered in the Categorization of Southern Politics." A significant "jig" in the Southern political jigsaw puzzle is the position of the Establishment. Where does it fit in the state's political picture? What is its position? The answer is not that which might be expected. Nor is it in accord with the popular conception of the role of the Southern Establishment; nor does it square with the belief held by this researcher at the beginning of the investigation.

More than a century after the Civil War, views of the South can be and often are as vigorous or fetid as the atmosphere of the Democratic Convention Hall in Charleston in 1860. There are those who subscribe to the traditions that the Lost Cause was holier than any grail sought by Galahad and that the forename of the Northern commander at Appomattox should be pronounced "Useless S." Others think of the twentieth-century South as a land of barbarians controlled by Bourbon aristocrats who are themselves tools of Northern capitalists, a land branded with brutality, permeated by poverty, tainted by corruption, and festooned with the Ku Klux Klan. With James Silver many believe that the South is a "Closed Society" based on a Southern power complex supporting racism and fanatical political conservatism. Both philosophies, unfortunately, have some of the patina of truth.

The mockingbirds still sing in the magnolia trees. Lee's ghostly veterans still march in all the bravery of butternut and gray down the dusty roads to Gettysburg. The Ku Kluxers, it is alleged, still lynch and burn and torture. Southern juries still free or give farcical sentences to murderers of white civil rights workers. In the words of Ralph McGill, white "friends" still say to their long-time Negro retainers:

Sam, them outside city niggers have got a bunch of those high school children all worked up and they are fixing to march again. Now I tell you what I want to do. I want you to leave the tractor settin' right there, and I want you to go back to the house and wash up and put on some clean clothes. Then I want you to go get Toby and Big Ed and some of the other good niggers around here. And I want you to stop this damn foolishness. . . . Tell 'em, by God, it ain't never goin' to change.[1]

[1] Ralph McGill, "A Confrontation in Dixie," *Louisville Times*, November 16, 1965, section B, p. 1.

Lester Maddox, John Bell Williams, and their like still stride through the halls of Southern governors' mansions.

On the other hand, and fortunately, both extremes are exaggerated, as this study may begin to indicate. Both the Lost Cause and the "Closed Society" belong at least partly in the realm of myth. The disciples of neither George Wallace nor Harriet Beecher Stowe reflect the complete picture. And the power structure, contrary to my original premise and contrary to Silver, does not necessarily endorse Southern gubernatorial conservatism, does not always support Silver's "Closed Society." In fact, as T. Harry Williams points out, "Southern politics is a morass of paradoxes, ambiguities, and incredible situations."[2] "The politics of the South," in the words of V. O. Key, Jr., "is incredibly complex."[3]

With the firmly held opinion that such Southern governors as George Wallace, Ross Barnett, Paul Johnson, and Earl Long were elected with and through the support of the Southern power structure, and that newspapers and the substantial business element supported conservative gubernatorial candidates of the type and philosophy of the above-named Southern statesmen, an exhaustive survey of recent gubernatorial elections in the three Southern states of Alabama, Mississippi, and Louisiana was conducted. The survey was limited to these states and for that reason is obviously incomplete. Alabama,

[2] T. Harry Williams, *Romance and Realism in Southern Politics*, p. ix.

[3] V. O. Key, Jr., *Southern Politics*, p. ix.

Mississippi, and Louisiana are, however, among the deep Southern or cotton states. Their opposition to changes in the last two decades, and especially since the decision in *Brown* v. *Board of Education*, has been, to put it mildly, spectacular and vehement. Their successful gubernatorial candidates have been outspoken and some of them picturesque. Key's excellent and definitive work on Southern politics stops in 1949; and, though based on experience and history, his intimated predictions that changes in the Deep South will drive "toward a Political system more completely in accord with the national ideas of constitutional morality"[4] have not materialized.

The chief medium of the research was through newspapers in the three states, Alabama, Mississippi, and Louisiana, supplemented by letters and personal interviews. A questionnaire was mailed to the editors and publishers of every daily newspaper and to a number of representative weekly and semi-weekly newspapers in the three states. The questionnaire was simple, and thus did not permit the investigation and development of subtleties and nuances that would have provided better and more complete conclusions. It was believed, however, that (1) more answers would be obtained if interrogations were brief, and (2) simple questions with a wide pattern of response would be more indicative of the state situation as a whole than a resort to hair-splitting, nit-picking, and obfuscated semantics. Admittedly, oversimplification of terms caused

4 Ibid., pp. v–675.

the responding editors difficulty. In fact, one, somewhat irritated, replied that the only way to get the true story would be to spend much time in all the towns in the three states, an inviting and desirable but somewhat impractical prospect.

Resort to the editors and publishers of newspapers was employed because it was believed that (1) newspapers generally represent one important element in the power structure of a community; (2) newspapers often reflect interests similar to the substantial business, advertising, and other leading elements of the community, and these, too, are important components of the community power matrix; and (3) newspapers, and particularly the political editors of newspapers, are familiar with local political conditions and atmosphere—more cognizant, perhaps, than any other groups except the traditional, so-called courthouse clique, and efforts to determine and elicit information from such courthouse sources proved unreliable.

The response of the newspaper editors and publishers was heartening and helpful. Every daily in Louisiana, all but one in Mississippi, and all but three in Alabama responded. The selected weekly and semiweekly newspapers were also cooperative. (In a few cities with more than one daily under common ownership, only one daily was polled.) Represented are the leading newspapers in the more significant cities and towns: twenty-three in Louisiana, twenty-five in Mississippi, and twenty-six in Alabama. This is a relatively complete sampling. Editors were candid and occasionally colorful in their comments. Although only one placed any limitation on the use of the material, none will be quoted directly. Without the help of newspapers, the survey would have been difficult and much more incomplete.

The editors were asked four questions:

1. In your state which of the two candidates in each of the last four Democratic primary runoffs, if either, did your newspaper support?

2. Which of the two candidates did the substantial community leadership support?

3. How would you classify the candidates? As Conservative? Moderate? Liberal?

4. What, in your opinion, were the chief issues in the campaigns?

A brief explanation of Questions Two and Three may be in order. Question One, "newspaper support," and Question Four, "issues," are obvious. In Question Two, the term "substantial community leadership" was defined as "the prominent citizens, business men, property owners, and other community leaders of your city and county." This is a relatively comprehensive and embracing term. Its weakness is that it does not necessarily include the so-called courthouse crowd, which may or may not be mythical. In Question Three, the term "Conservative" was defined generally as "(a) opposition to the 'welfare state,' (b) opposition to integration, and (c) support of States' rights." The term "Liberal" was defined generally as "(a) support of the 'welfare state,' (b) support of or silence on integration, and (c) a belief in expanding the powers of the federal government." The term "Moderate" was defined as "a position somewhere between the designations 'Conservative' and 'Liberal' or silence or evasion."

The past four gubernatorial elections in each of the three states were analyzed: in Alabama, the elections of 1954, 1958, 1962, and 1966; in Louisiana, the elections of 1956, 1960, 1964, and 1967 (actually, primaries are held in Louisiana at the fag end of the preceding year, but runoffs stretch over into the even-numbered years); and in Mississippi, the elections of 1955, 1959, 1963, and 1967.

Since the survivors in each election defeated the Republican candidates in the November elections with relative ease, attention has been concentrated largely on the Democratic runoff primaries. The prospects of the South's becoming a two-party section are beyond the province of the investigation. Those prospects have been considered in great detail by a number of historians, political scientists, and publicists, among them Dewey W. Grantham, V. O. Key, Jr., W. H. Nicholls, Charles O. Lerche, R. J. Steamer, Donald S. Strong, Phillip E. Converse, Allan P. Sindler, James R. Soukup, Clifton McCleskey, and Harry Holloway.[5] This is a survey of state primaries. The

5 D. W. Grantham, *The Democratic South*, pp. 42–98; Key, *Southern Politics*, pp. v–675; W. H. Nicholls, *Southern Tradition and Regional Progress*, pp. 73–101; Charles O. Lerche, *The Uncertain South*, pp. 218 ff.; Allan P. Sindler, ed., *Change in the Contemporary South*, pp. 150–238; James R. Soukup, Clifton McCleskey, and Harry Holloway, *Party and Factional Division in Texas*, pp. 3–182.

antic behavior of the Southern states in recent national presidential elections is also beyond the province of the investigation.

One curiosity of Southern gubernatorial elections is the custom of encores or repeat performances. The chief candidates run again and again. Although Alabama and Mississippi have provisions against immediate gubernatorial succession, the same names are found repeatedly on ballots. Thus, from the standpoint of providing a number of new faces in the sweepstakes, Silver was correct. In that sense the South is a "Closed Society."

The runoff candidates in the elections in the various states were:

*Alabama*

    1954: James E. Folsom against the Bay Minette newspaper publisher, James Faulkner, with Folsom the winner.

    1958: John Patterson against Circuit Judge George Wallace with Patterson the winner.

    1962: George Wallace against Ryan de Graffenreid, with Wallace the winner. De Graffenreid had barely edged out J. E. Folsom in the primary.

    1966: Lurleen Wallace, now deceased, wife of Governor George Wallace, against a star-studded field of Alabama politicians that included almost everyone except "Bear" Bryant and the Ten Commandments. Such was the magic of the Wallace name (or possibly because her leading

opponent was killed in an airplane crash) that Mrs.
Wallace won without a runoff.

*Louisiana*

1956: deLesseps Morrison against E. K. Long, brother of
the assassinated Huey, with Long the winner.

1960: deLesseps Morrison against Jimmie Davis, author of
"You Are My Sunshine," with Davis the winner.

1964: deLesseps Morrison against J. J. McKeithan, with
McKeithan the winner.

1967: J. J. McKeithan against John R. Rarick. McKeithan
won without a runoff.

In a sense, the 1966 Alabama and the 1967 Louisiana elections
are oddities and distort the general pattern of the findings.
They are oddities because in each election a candidate fore-
ordained to victory from the beginning won without a runoff
—Mrs. Wallace in Alabama and John McKeithan in Louisiana. The campaign of Mrs. Wallace was further strengthened
by the fact that the candidate presumed to be her strongest
opponent, Ryan de Graffenreid, was killed before the campaign actually got off the ground. Thus answers to the ques-
tionnaires in these two elections may have been weighted, since
it is not the practice of newspapers or the power structure
state-wide openly to oppose an obvious winner. However, the
sum total of the weighted response in these two cases more or
less balanced out, since Mrs. Wallace was considered in Alabama to be a Conservative and McKeithan in Louisiana, by

1967, a Moderate. The third recent election, that of Mississippi in 1967, followed the pattern of preceeding elections.

*Mississippi*

> 1955: J. P. Coleman against P. B. Johnson, with Coleman
> the winner.
> 1959: Ross Barnett against Carroll Gartin, with Barnett the
> winner.
> 1963: Coleman against P. B. Johnson as in 1955, but with
> Johnson the winner.
> 1967: John Bell Williams against William Winter, with
> Williams the winner.

The results of the questionnaire on newspaper support,
substantial community leadership support, and classification
are found, state by state, in Table I. Although that table may
well bear careful study, space does not permit individual com-
ment, election by election and state by state. Some observations
on the issues in the individual elections, however, follow. Let
us first look at Alabama.

In the Alabama Democratic gubernatorial campaign of
1954, there were no major issues. Fundamentally the election
was a clash of personalities, the colorful Folsom against the
more sedate Faulkner. Folsom, a Liberal, borrowed a page
from the tactics of Conservative W. Lee O'Daniel ("Pass the
biscuits, Pappy") of Texas fame, campaigning with a string
band and passing out buckets for contributions. The strategy
proved successful.[6] As one Alabama editor explained the re-

[6] *New York Times*, May 2, 1954, p. 63; May 6, 1954, p. 38.

sults, "Folsom promised more things to more people—education, old age pensions—and more people believed him."

In the Alabama election of 1958 the extraneous factor of sympathy rather than conservatism played an important role, since both candidates, Patterson and Wallace, were Conservatives. Patterson, as one macabre Alabama journalist commented, "rode to victory on the coattails of his dead father," the attorney general elect who was assassinated while attempting to break up an alleged vice ring in Phoenix City. The Patterson success justified in part the cynical observation that it is virtually impossible in the South to win a race from a cripple, a blind man, or a martyr. Political classification of the two was identical, with seventeen newspapers terming each candidate as Conservative, and four as Moderate. It requires imagination to regard either or both of the stalwart States' righters Patterson and Wallace as Liberal, but four Alabama newspapers managed to accomplish it, presumably on the basis that both were tainted with mild vestiges of Populism.

Issues in the 1958 election were blurred. One editor stated that Wallace himself explained his defeat in the classic words, "Patterson out-segged me." If this was true, it was not a mistake that Judge Wallace was to permit himself again. According to the *New York Times*, Wallace claimed that Patterson was supported by the Ku Klux Klan and that Grand Dragon Robert Shelton was a friend of Patterson. Whatever the issues, Patterson won by 64,000 votes.[7] Patterson was

[7] Ibid., May 8, 1958, p. 21; June 4, 1958, p. 16; June 5, 1958, p. 20.

# TABLE I

## Newspaper and Substantial Community Leadership Support and Classification

### ALABAMA

| | 1954 | | | 1958 | | | 1962 | | | | 1966 | |
|---|---|---|---|---|---|---|---|---|---|---|---|---|
| | Folsom Elected | Faulkner | None or Other | Patterson Elected | Wallace | None or Other | Folsom | de Graffenreid | Wallace Elected | None or Other | L. Wallace Elected | All Opponents |
| Newspapers supporting | 1 | 10 | 13 | 7 | 8 | 10 | 0 | 11 | 8 | 6 | 9 | 8 |
| Substantial community leadership supporting | 7 | 12 | 2 Split 3 Other | 17 | 6 | 2 Split | 0 | 9 | 12 | 4 Split | 13 | 4 |
| Classified by newspapers as: | | | | | | | | | | | | |
| Conservative | 5 | 3 | — | 17 | 17 | — | 4 | 2 | 20 | — | 16 | 10 |
| Moderate | 4 | 15 | — | 4 | 4 | — | 4 | 18 | 1 | — | 2 | 20 |
| Liberal | 14 | 6 | — | 4 | 4 | — | 15 | 5 | 5 | — | 2 | 33 |

### LOUISIANA

| | 1956 | | | 1960 | | | 1964 | | | 1967 | | |
|---|---|---|---|---|---|---|---|---|---|---|---|---|
| | Long Elected | Morrison | None or Other | Davis Elected | Morrison | None or Other | McKeithan Elected | Morrison | None or Other | McKeithan Elected | Rarick | None or Other |
| Newspapers supporting | 1 | 8 | 13 None 1 Other | 2 | 8 | 13 None 0 Other | 1 | 9 | 11 None 2 Other | 16 | 0 | 15 None 1 Other |

| | | | | | | | | | | | | |
|---|---|---|---|---|---|---|---|---|---|---|---|---|
| Substantial community leadership supporting | 7 | 9 | 2 Split 3 Other | 7 | 12 | 1 Split 2 Other | 5 | 14 | 1 Split 2 Other | 33 | 0 | 1 None 0 Other |
| Classified by newspapers as: | | | | | | | | | | | | |
| Conservative | 2 | 1 | — | 12 | 1 | — | 9 | 1 | — | 2 | 27 | — |
| Moderate | 4 | 8 | — | 8 | 8 | — | 10 | 8 | — | 27 | 0 | — |
| Liberal | 14 | 13 | — | 0 | 13 | — | 1 | 13 | — | 0 | 0 | — |

MISSISSIPPI

| | 1955 | | | 1959 | | | 1963 | | | 1967 | |
|---|---|---|---|---|---|---|---|---|---|---|---|
| | Coleman Elected | Johnson | None or Other | Barnett Elected | Gartin | None or Other | Johnson | Coleman | None or Other | Williams Elected | Winter |
| Newspapers supporting | 13 | 5 | 4 | 5 | 13 | 4 | 9 | 11 | 2 None 1 Repub. | 13 | 8 |
| Substantial community leadership supporting | 13 | 6 | 1 Split | 10 | 9 | 4 Split | 11 | 9 | 2 Split 2 Repub. | 6 | 14 |
| Classified by newspapers as: | | | | | | | | | | | |
| Conservative | 10 | 16 | — | 19 | 10 | — | 18 | 7 | — | 25 | 1 |
| Moderate | 9 | 3 | — | 2 | 11 | — | 3 | 14 | — | 1 | 23 |
| Liberal | 1 | 1 | — | 0 | 0 | — | 1 | 2 | — | 0 | 4 |

among those to be decisively defeated by Mrs. Lurleen Wallace in the election of 1966.

The 1962 election in Alabama reveals a shift, an unsuccessful shift, toward moderation on the part of the Alabama power structure. A substantial segment supported the more moderate Ryan de Graffenreid, who lost by about 53,000 votes.[8] Eleven newspapers, including some of the big city dailies, were in the de Graffenreid camp. Eight in the smaller towns leaned to Wallace. None supported J. E. Folsom, barely defeated by de Graffenreid in the first primary for a place in the runoff. Nor was the "better" community leadership preponderantly for Wallace, though he had the support of twelve of the polled communities to nine for de Graffenreid and none for Folsom. As in the case of the newspapers, the power structure in the smaller communities supported Wallace, whereas that in the large communities either liked de Graffenreid or was split. Wallace was overwhelmingly termed Conservative; one Alabama editor classified him as "Neanderthal."

The issue in the 1962 race in the consensus of most Alabama editors was clear-cut: Wallace supported segregation and defied the federal government, whereas de Graffenreid was more moderate on the racial issue and was tarred with the brush of being more attuned to the national Democratic party. This view was shared by the *New York Times*.[9] Indicative of possible change in the South was one influential editor's frank

[8] Ibid., May 30, 1962, p. 6.
[9] Ibid., May 3, 1962, p. 23; May 5, 1962, p. 18.

confession: "Our support [of Wallace] was based on the Wallace support of a liberal education program and a belief that his segregation stand was a pose which would be dropped once he was elected. Except in education he has been a total disappointment."[10]

The 1966 Alabama election was, as has been indicated earlier, a free-for-all. A number of candidates opposed Mrs. Wallace, whose campaign was spearheaded by her husband, George. George wanted to succeed himself but was prohibited from doing so by the Alabama constitution. Borrowing from the experience of "Farmer" Jim Ferguson, former impeached governor of Texas who successfully ran his wife, Miriam A. ("Ma"), for the highest office in the state, George offered the services of his spouse instead. The opposition was split a number of ways. The Wallaces benefited not only from the death of a leading opponent, but also, according to some cynical newspaper correspondents, from a grave error perpetrated by another leading opponent, the dynamic Richmond Flowers, then attorney general of Alabama. Richmond, Junior, a star hurdler and halfback, unfortunately pursued his search for higher learning at the University of Tennessee, and we do not let a good Alabama athlete get out of Alabama and still stay popular with the sovereign voters of that great state. The issue in the 1966 Alabama race, according to most Alabama newspapers, was racism, racism not so pure but very simple. Some

[10] Ibid., May 9, 1962, p. 24.

newspapers, however, especially those that supported the Wallaces, said with some piety that the issue and the basis of their support for Mrs. Wallace was Wallace's "excellent" economic record in Alabama. One Alabama editor, borrowing perhaps unconsciously from the theme song of the musical *Damn Yankees* (the title of which should be popular in Alabama), "Whatever Lola Wants, Lola Gets," summed up the issues concisely by stating, "What George says goes in Alabama, right or wrong." Mrs. Wallace won without a runoff. It is perhaps significant, however, even in this emotion-packed race and despite the allegation, false or true, that newspapers opposing the Wallaces simply did not get lucrative state advertising contracts, that (1) a number of Alabama newspapers refused to endorse any candidate, and (2) almost as many newspapers opposed as supported the Wallace candidacy. The ratio was nine newspaper endorsements for Mrs. Wallace to eight for her various opponents—and many newspapers had endorsed the now dead de Graffenreid in a previous election.

The Alabama elections have been considered. Louisiana, too, has had some interesting gubernatorial elections. A survey of the most recent follows.

Since deLesseps ("Chep") Morrison was a runoff candidate in the first three elections surveyed, the results may be grouped. The majority of the newspapers indicating a choice supported Morrison in all three races—eight to one over Long, eight to two against Davis, and nine to one against McKeithan. (The usually accurate *New York Times'* statement that every major newspaper in the state except those in Baton Rouge supported Davis is in error.[11] Although the two that backed Davis were important, many others favored Morrison.)

Although not as favorable toward him as the newspapers, the substantial community element generally leaned toward Morrison: nine to seven against Long, twelve to seven against Davis, and fourteen to five against McKeithan. It may be noted that in 1964 at least two of the more significant newspapers and several business communities supported the Republican candidate Lyons in the November election.

Morrison was definitely regarded as more moderate or liberal than either Davis or McKeithan. Some editors had difficulty in terminology, one classifying Long as "crazy," and another Davis as "Ugh!" It is not known under which political philosophy those designations would properly fit.

There was a remarkable consensus among the editors upon the issues involved in the first three campaigns. Not necessarily listed in the order of importance, the issues were (1) North Louisiana against South Louisiana and the "New Orleans machine"; (2) (closely allied with the first) the "country boy" image of Long and Davis against the "city slicker" Morrison; (3) Protestantism versus Morrison's Catholicism; and, in the Davis and McKeithan campaigns, (4) race and the national party, probably the most significant issues of all. Morrison was far more moderate on integration than either Davis

[11] Ibid., January 11, 1960, p. 30.

or McKeithan and much more in accord with the national party.[12]

There were other facets listed by various editors, such as "the power of the Long adherents," "demagoguery versus statesmanship," and better and harder campaigning by Long and McKeithan.

Both Earl Long and Jimmie Davis were more colorful than either Morrison or McKeithan. Although Earl Long did not have all of the vigor of his brother (one Louisianian referred to him as "the Kingfish filleted, with neither the backbone nor the spleen of old Huey"),[13] still he had his moments. Davis was almost as picturesque. One observer described him as "an upstate sharecropper's son who has parlayed his baritone voice and a talent for writing hill-billy songs and his business ability into a sizable fortune."[14] Davis was fairly well educated as current Southern politicians go, with a Master of Arts degree in psychology and education. He was the Pelican State's "Sunshine" in two different gubernatorial administrations.

McKeithan, personable but solemn, was an unexpected victor in the 1964 election. A *New York Times* analysis immediately prior to the election did not list him as a possible prospect for the runoff.[15] That he made it at all was an upset; in the first primary Morrison led him by 140,000 votes, usually

12 Ibid., December 9, 1963, p. 1.
13 Ibid., January 22, 1956, part IV, p. 2.
14 Ibid.
15 Ibid., December 3, 1963, p. 75.

a comfortable margin.[16] In the runoff McKeithan emerged the victor by approximately 40,000 votes.[17]

In a postelection analysis, Claude Sitton of the *New York Times* flatly predicted that the success of McKeithan would result in increased hostility to the Negro and civil rights.[18] The *New York Times* was wrong. McKeithan has adopted a moderate position on integration. In fact, he has demonstrated an unusual amount of courage for a Southern politician. In the Bogalusa incidents, he has stood repeatedly for law and order and against local anarchy. A number of Louisiana newspaper editors who had opposed McKeithan commented in the questionnaire that he is proving to be a pleasant surprise and is making an excellent governor. Thus we have antithetical situations in the cases of Wallace of Alabama and McKeithan of Louisiana. As has been suggested, an Alabama editor thought that Wallace's defiance of the federal government was a pose that would be dropped. It was not. Some Louisiana editors believed that McKeithan's defiance of the federal government would be in the tradition of Wallace and Barnett of Mississippi. Instead, it apparently was a pose and was dropped. For example, in the most recent election analyzed, that of December, 1967, virtually all of the newspaper editors classified McKeithan as a Moderate; only about one-half of them so classified him four years earlier in the election of 1963–1964.

16 Ibid., December 9, 1963, p. 1.
17 Ibid., January 13, 1964, p. 16.
18 Ibid., p. 13.

Conversely, all termed McKeithan's opponent Rarick a Conservative. The issues generally were industrial progress and
McKeithan's moderate stand on integration. Editors and publishers did not regard the 1967 joust as much of a contest; one
called it a "nil-non race," another described it as a "walk
rather than a race," and a third as "the quietest, dullest race I
have ever seen in Louisiana." McKeithan received more than
80 percent of the votes.

Shifting from Louisiana to Mississippi, one finds that in
each of the four Mississippi elections surveyed the fundamental
question was the degree of conservatism exhibited or to be
expected in action on integration and civil rights. The claim is
not made that any leader or Mississippi candidate was a Liberal
on the race issue. Far from it. The Moderate Coleman pledged
himself to eternal enforcement of segregation. The Moderate
Gartin was a member of the White Citizens' Councils, that
Ku Klux Klan with deodorants. To assume any other position
in the Mississippi of the twentieth century was to invite quick
and early political oblivion. But—and this is important—there
were degrees of fanaticism on the racial question. The more
moderate of the Mississippi Conservatives did not, in the eyes
of the voters, think that it was true what they say about Dixie;
they did not really mean to bar the door to the ingress of the
black despotism of the North that would come seeking to drag
Mississippi willy-nilly into the United States. Moderate conservatism was not enough. The majority of Mississippi voters
wanted—the Mississippi voters, not the Mississippi power

structure—a King Canute who could stand at the shore and bid the waves roll back. Repeating the statement of McGill's Southern owner to his Negro tenant, they vowed, "By God, it ain't never goin' to change around here." And in their mysticism—or idiocy—they thought their Barnetts and Paul Johnsons and John Bell Williamses could roll back the twentieth century, come hell, high water, the federal marshals, the United States Marines, or even Bobby Kennedy.

This is not necessarily an aberration confined to the state of Mississippi. In the more moderate Texas of March, 1966, highly prominent Texas officials of both parties were, in the pithy words of Ralph Yarborough, United States senator from Texas, "squalling to high heavens"[19] against the Federal Bureau of Investigation and the federal Department of Justice for having the audacity to attempt to investigate voter registration in their sacred confines. Just a few years ago the eminent Texas cowboy-historian J. Evetts Haley, comrade-in-arms to General Edwin Walker, ran for governor on a ticket of interposition, or, as he phrased it, "We'll meet the federal marshals at the Red River with the Texas Rangers." Unlike Mississippi protectors of the States' rights concept, however, staunch Texas segregationist Haley ran dismally in his gubernatorial sweepstakes, and some wag observed that every Texas Ranger voted against him.

Did the Mississippi power structure share the sentiments of

[19] *Fort Worth Star-Telegram* (Evening), March 5, 1966, section 1, p. 5.

the Mississippi voter in the elections of 1955, 1959, 1963, and 1967? The answer is both "yes" and "no," but more "no" than "yes," as may be seen from Table I. In all three elections, the total newspaper and other community leadership support was substantially for the more moderate candidate.

Mississippi issues in the elections were plain and simple—race, segregation, and the national Democratic party. As one Mississippi newspaper editor plaintively observed, "There are seldom any new issues in Mississippi." There were, of course, variations on the ancient theme in each of the elections. Coleman in 1955, according to some editors, was a fresher face, more able, a better manager, more qualified to bring industrialization to Mississippi, and possibly supported by the more popular former governors. In 1959 Barnett, who was classified politically by one Mississippi newspaper editor as "incredible," was more inflammatory than Gartin, and Mississippi voters wanted a fire. The 1963 election was probably the most interesting, since it followed the Meredith–University of Mississippi incident, and since it was a reversal of the 1955 election. Most editors agreed that Johnson benefited from his heroic stand in attempting to shield the spires of Oxford from the droppings of the senegambians, and thus to the voters seemed to substantiate the Johnson vow "to work for the defeat of the dark forces of Federal control and regimentation."[20] Coleman, hung, as one editor phrased it, with the Kennedy albatross which he attempted to disavow, pledged "peace and tran-

[20] *New York Times*, August 29, 1963, p. 12.

quility," a pledge that Johnson termed "a mockingbird in the magnolia tree,"[21] whatever that means. Coleman made a salient attack on the Johnson–Ole Miss heroics—an attack, however, not appealing to the majority of the Mississippi voters—when he described Johnson's barring the door of the University of Mississippi to James Meredith and the federal marshals somewhat as follows:

Johnson raised his fist.

The fist went down.

Meredith went in.[22]

This was a hardheaded look at the hopelessness of the attempts of the rednecks, the Barnetts, and the Eastlands to stem the tide of the future and forever to thwart the will of much of the rest of the United States, but it was not a look to elicit tender glances from the Mississippi voter. Coleman was defeated in 1963 by a vote of approximately 217,000 to 162,000.[23]

The cold chill winds of federal interposition are, however, being felt in Mississippi also. P. B. Johnson in his 1964–1968 term of office, like McKeithan in Louisiana, although he did not approve change, accepted it, and, in a sense, yielded to it, becoming in office much more moderate than had been anticipated. One editor, commenting on the change, added, ". . . and we are delighted." Others stated that the main issue was civil rights, and one added, apparently with a sense of relief,

21 Ibid., August 8, 1963, p. 17.
22 Ibid.
23 Ibid., August 28, 1963, p. 28.

". . . for the last time in Mississippi." He was, however, op-
timistic. In the 1967, or most recent, Mississippi gubernatorial
primary, the Moderate William Winter (who was actually
much more liberal than some of his Moderate predecessors)
opposed John Bell Williams, who had been deprived of his
Democratic congressional seniority rights because of his
staunch support of Republican Barry Goldwater in the presidential election of 1964. One Mississippi newspaper editor
expressed the issue of 1967 as "redneck know-nothings versus
enlightened progress." Williams defeated Winter, whom he
had successfully labeled "a Kennedy-Johnson Liberal," by
more than 60,000 votes. Williams then staved off the challenge of the Republican Rubel Phillips in the general election.
(Would Rubel have been more successful if he had changed
the *u* in his first name to an *e?*) The Republican Phillips was
generally classified as a Moderate, though one editor somewhat sourly remarked, "Hell, he didn't know himself what he
was." An irony of the election, considering the wholehearted
support given by Williams to the Republican Goldwater in
1964, was to find the same Williams declaiming in 1967, as
quoted by W. F. Minor in the conservative New Orleans
*Times-Picayune*, that the last Republican governor of the state,
General Adelbert Ames, "was enough for 100 years"[24] and
joining United States Senator James Eastland, who declared
that "we must pick the political bones of this crowd [the

[24] W. F. Minor, "Eyes on Mississippi," *Times-Picayune* (New
Orleans), November 5, 1967, section 2, p. 7.

Republicans] that would destroy Mississippi." Mississippi statesmen are men of high principle.

It is possible (if some semicomic relief may be interjected into these notes of racial conflict and gloom) that Mississippi governors may have new focal points of attack other than federal marshals, the Republicans, and the national Democratic party—to wit, the Jackson gendarmes. In fact, one such shift in emphasis transpired during the recent administration of Governor Paul Johnson. Mississippi was until recently the only prohibition state that taxed bootleggers. Some Mississippi statesmen were accused either justly or unjustly of voting "dry" and drinking "wet." Liquor allegedly flowed free in some of Jackson's better clubs and, shockingly enough, almost in sight of the state's Confederate Capitol. During Johnson's administration, Jackson's "finest" raided an exclusive soiree at which the governor was allegedly in attendance and hauled off some of the younger members of the upper crust, the power structure, to the pokey. The Mississippi legislature immediately thereafter repealed prohibition in Mississippi. Thus "Time Marches On" and progress is being made down on the Delta. Political winds do shift.

Thus far, twelve elections in three states have been surveyed. The candidates, their success or failure, their political complexion, newspaper and substantial community leadership support, and the issues have been considered.

With the above classifications presented, the overall totals are summarized in Tables II, III, and IV. Newspaper and

## TABLE II

### Conservative and Moderate Support by States

| ALABAMA | | | | | LOUISIANA | | | | | MISSISSIPPI | | | | |
|---|---|---|---|---|---|---|---|---|---|---|---|---|---|---|
| Year | Newspaper Support | | Substantial Community Leadership Support | | Year | Newspaper Support | | Substantial Community Leadership Support | | Year | Newspaper Support | | Substantial Community Leadership Support | |
| | More Cons. Cand. | More Mod. Cand. | More Cons. Cand. | More Mod. Cand. | | More Cons. Cand. | More Mod. Cand. | More Cons. Cand. | More Mod. Cand. | | More Cons. Cand. | More Mod. Cand. | More Cons. Cand. | More Mod. Cand. |
| 1954 | 10 | 1 | 12 | 7 | 1956 | 1 | 8 | 7 | 9 | 1955 | 5 | 13 | 6 | 13 |
| 1958 | No real degree of difference in conservatism | | | | 1960 | 2 | 8 | 7 | 12 | 1959 | 5 | 13 | 10 | 9 |
| 1962 | 8 | 11 | 12 | 9 | 1964 | 1 | 9 | 5 | 14 | 1963 | 9 | 11 | 11 | 9 |
| 1966 | 9 | 8 | 13 | 4 | 1968 | 0 | 16 | 0 | 33 | 1967 | 8 | 14 | 6 | 14 |
| TOTALS | 27 | 20 | 37 | 20 | | 4 | 41 | 19 | 68 | | 27 | 51 | 33 | 45 |

## TABLE III

### Grand Total: Conservative and Moderate Support

| State | Newspaper Support | | Substantial Community Leadership Support | |
|---|---|---|---|---|
| | The More Conservative Candidate | The More Moderate Candidate | The More Conservative Candidate | The More Moderate Candidate |
| Alabama | 27 | 20 | 37 | 20 |
| Louisiana | 4 | 41 | 19 | 68 |
| Mississippi | 27 | 51 | 33 | 45 |
| TOTALS | 58 | 112 | 89 | 133 |

## TABLE IV

### Influence of Support by Newspaper and Substantial Community Elements: 12 Elections

| Newspaper | | Substantial Community Element | |
|---|---|---|---|
| Majority of Newspapers Supported the Winner | Majority of Newspapers Supported the Loser | Majority of Community Element Supported the Winner | Majority of Community Element Supported the Loser |
| 3 | 9 | 7 | 5 |

substantial community leadership support are shown state by
state in Table II. Grand totals are presented in Table III. The
success and failure of such support is shown in Table IV.
Especially significant are the results in Tables II and III.

The overall totals in Table III are surprising. Contrary to
the original hypothesis, the summary shows that newspapers
in the three states were decidedly in favor of the more moderate candidates, by the significant total of 112 to 58. The substantial leadership in the community, other than newspapers,
was more closely divided, but here too the vote was in favor of
the moderate candidate, 133 to 89. In brief, approximately
60 percent of the substantial leadership in an extensive community sampling in three Southern states that, with the possible
exception of Arkansas, have been most aggressive in resisting
integration and civil rights supported the more racially moderate candidates. Discounting the overwhelming community support given to the Moderate McKeithan of Louisiana in the
1967 election, which is somewhat counterbalanced by support
for the Conservative Mrs. Wallace in the Alabama election of
1966, and throwing those freak elections out completely, still
approximately 54 percent of the power structure supported the
more moderate candidate.

If newspapers are part of the Southern power structure, if
newspaper editors and publishers are aware of the political
sentiments of the leadership within their respective communities, and if the newspaper reports are correct, and there is every
reason to believe that they are, then the power structure does

not offer majority support to gubernatorial conservatism, and the three states are not quite Silver's "Closed Society." If these data are true, earlier and excellent conclusions no longer hold true. The winds are indeed shifting.

An interesting side issue is shown in Table IV, "Influence of Support." The newspapers backed a winner in only three of the twelve elections, the almost automatic and sentiment-filled campaign of Patterson in Alabama in 1958 and the fore-ordained Alabama and Louisiana elections of 1967. Numerically, the community leadership were better pickers, the majority of the communities' power structures supporting the victor in seven of the twelve elections and the loser in five. These totals, however, are deceiving, because a slight shift in the totals of individual communities' power structure support would have thrown this group into the ranks of those who selected losers in almost the same proportion as both newspaper and total support. Only in Alabama did the newspapers and the power structure support the more conservative candidate. Here the statistics may have been misleadingly swelled by the support for Faulkner, no rabid segregationist of the Wallace genre, against Folsom, definitely not the type to appeal to any power structure, regardless of his stand on race, and by the support given to Mrs. Wallace, an obvious winner. Newspapers generally in these three states seem not to carry the same political impact as do the newspapers of Texas, which are often found on the side of the winning angels.

Since the newspapers by a total vote of 112 to 58 and the

substantial community leadership by a vote of 132 to 89 supported the Moderates, from whence came the votes for Barnett,
Wallace, Johnson, Davis, and Williams? If the analysis is
correct, it did not come from the community power structure,
the upper middle class as represented by the newspapers and
other community leaders. If this is true, then one conclusion
of the scholarly John Dollard in his comprehensive sociological
study of caste in a Southern town no longer holds true: that the
poorer whites show less than the predicted resentment of
Negroes and the middle-class whites much more.[25] Dollard
quotes middle-class Negroes as authority for the belief that the
chief hostility between white and Negro comes from what
are termed "strainers," the middle-class whites who are "strain-
ing" to better their positions by stepping on the Negro. The
findings of this survey do not show that position to be correct.

Nor do the findings support the conclusion of W. J. Cash
that the solidly conservative political hierarchies are being
increasingly dominated by "the new industrial and commercial
magnates."[26] More correct, perhaps, is another Cash conclusion,
that the political hierarchies are still controlled to a great ex-
tent by the planter class—for example, Senator James Eastland
of Mississippi—motivated possibly by a desire for the reten-
tion of cheap labor.

The findings are also at variance with the V. O. Key statement that "it is the poorer whites who support candidates

[25] John Dollard, *Caste and Class in a Southern Town*, p. 58.
[26] W. J. Cash, *The Mind of the South*, p. 249.

favoring governmental policies for the reduction of racial discriminations and for the alleviation of racial tensions."[27]

Directly consonant with the findings of this study are the conclusions of Lerche that the responsibility for the defeat of the racial moderates (among whom he erroneously numbers the White Citizens' Councils) falls not on the conservative power structure but on the "poor whites led by the militant demagogues."[28] Nicholls agrees, stating that rural prejudices, "especially on matters of race, have a weight far in excess of the relative number of voters."[29] The demagogues find handy enemies, ranging from Dwight Eisenhower through Chief Justice Warren to any candidate who opposes them for the governorship. Conversely, heroes fit to occupy niches beside Lee and Jackson as defenders of the Lost Cause are the Faubuses, the Barnetts, and the Wallaces, possibly even more heroic than Lee and Jackson, because the generals often won battles against "Those People" (Lee's reference to the Union commanders), but Barnett, Faubus, and Wallace never do.

Unquestionably there has been strenuous opposition to change in the South, and the modern heroes just mentioned have manned the ramparts valiantly, if unsuccessfully, against such change. Ours is a South of pride and prejudice, and many people want it to stay that way—for example, the eminent Southern historian Robert S. Cotterill, who closed his

---

27 Key, *Southern Politics*, p. 671.
28 Lerche, *The Uncertain South*, p. 243.
29 Nicholls, *Southern Tradition and Regional Progress*, pp. 92–93.

presidential address to the Southern Historical Association in 1949 with these words: "There is no Old South and no New. There is only the South. Fundamentally as it was in the beginning it is now, and, if God please, it shall be forevermore."[30] To which some historians might like to add the appendage, "God forbid!"

It is presumed that Professor Cotterill may have been thinking of the South of A.D. 2000 as pictured by Barnwell Rhett at the time of the South Carolina secession of 1860 and as quoted by Vann Woodward:

And extending their empire across this continent to the Pacific and down through Mexico to the other side of the great gulf and over the isles of the sea they [the South] established an empire and wrought out a civilization which has never been equalled or surpassed—a civilization teeming with orators, poets, philosophers, statesmen, and historians equal to those of Greece and Rome—and presented to the world the glorious spectacle of a free, prosperous, and illustrious people.[31]

To quote another eminent comedian, George Gobel, "you don't hardly find them kind any more," especially on a drive between Vicksburg and Monroe, Louisiana, or in West Dallas, Texas.

This Rhett mythology constitutes, as Sellers suggests, the

[30] R. S. Cotterill, "The Old South to the New," in *The Pursuit of Southern History*, ed. G. B. Tindall, p. 238.

[31] C. Vann Woodward, "The Irony of Southern History," in *Pursuit of Southern History*, ed. Tindall, p. 288.

tragedy of the South.[32] It is a tragedy worse, perhaps, than Appomattox, a tragedy to which, it is hoped, the second half of the twentieth century is writing finis.

This is the South that by and large and at least until the 1950's has been content to stew in its own juices, to resent outside interference, and to think that all is well with the world, certain that if evil did exist, some magic abracadabra or incantation would conjure up a Pollyanna or Elsie Dinsmore or Lydia Pinkham wearing, of course, a gray bonnet and a colonel's goatee to extricate the South from its own morass. That was the position of a number of Southern Liberals, William Faulkner and John Temple Graves, to name but two. Graves proclaimed that "the Negro problem is one on which the South can be stimulated into doing right things but not forced. . . . It is to these Southerners [Liberals] that leadership must be left."[33]

But leadership has not been left to these Liberals or Moderates or even moderate Conservatives because, by and large, as this survey shows, they have not generally supported the winning candidate. If they did support the winning candidate, they have been rewarded at times with leaders who permitted and encouraged Little Rocks, Oxfords, and Selmas.

The leadership has come; but in the recent past it has come from outside, armed with bayonets. Southern leadership, supported by the increasingly moderate power structure, is beginning to change, as is evidenced by the changing positions of

[32] Charles G. Sellers, Jr., ed., *The Southerner as American*, p. vi.
[33] John Temple Graves, *The Fighting South*, p. 161.

Governors Faubus, McKeithan, and Paul Johnson. The change
has not come through them, however, nor through the idealistic dreams of John Temple Graves and his fellow Southerners of good will who hope for voluntary reformation from
within, but, as L. D. Reddick points out, ". . . by the way of
national rather than regional or local attitudes and policies,"[34]
ranging from the abolition of slavery in the 1860's to the
Supreme Court's support of the Voter Registration Act and
Attorney General Nicholas Katzenbach's sending the alien
hirelings from Federal Bureau of Investigation into Texas to
check Texas voter registration in March, 1966.

The change is, however, occurring despite the last desperate
Confederate yells of the 1960's. The yells may contain the old
number of decibels. They do not have the same fearsome results. Governors McKeithan and Johnson may not even mean
the words. Keith McKean quotes John Ed Pearce of the
*Louisville Courier-Journal* on the Asheville Southern Governors' Conference, and agrees: ". . . The Words are not the
old words. They [the governors] may cling to the myth of the
Old South . . . but they know the excitement of the realities of
the present. . . . You got the feeling that they are beginning to
like the reality more than the myth."[35]

It may be well that, despite their protests, the Southern
political leaders are slowly learning to listen to the new South-

[34] L. D. Reddick, "The Negro as Southerner and American, in *The
Southerner as American*, ed. Sellers, p. 134.
[35] Keith F. McKean, *Cross Currents in the South*, pp. 49–50.

ern power structure, which may be willing to welcome the Yankee dollar on our sacred soil. That strange Alabamian W. H. Skaggs, in his curious book *The Southern Oligarchy*, written back in 1924, among other bitter indictments said that in many Southern towns the poorest public buildings were the schoolhouses and the best ones the jails. Southern leaders, at least many of them, are wanting the schoolhouse to take precedence over the jail. They are wanting better schoolhouses. They are, of course, wanting better jails. They are wanting new factories humming with the production of supplies, even if those supplies are sold to federal contractors. They might, though certainly no venality could be involved, welcome another federal architectural phenomenon, the federal pork barrel.

Thus, as Nicholls has suggested, the South must choose between tradition and progress.[36] Some of the leaders, in the words of Senator Ralph Yarborough of Texas, "are having to be dragged kicking and screaming into the twentieth century." Because of what Professor Thomas Clark terms "the deeply ingrained and reactionary nature of much political leadership . . . the new forces have been slow to revolt against the past."[37]

The revolt, however, if the results of this survey are correct, is occurring. Like Faulkner's insignificant man, it speaks thus far with puny voice, almost silenced by the drums of the

[36] Nicholls, *Southern Tradition and Regional Progress*, p. ix.
[37] T. D. Clark, "The South in Cultural Change," in *Change in the Contemporary South*, ed. Sindler, pp. 22–23.

demagogues. But it does speak, and we hope that like Faulkner's man it will speak inexhaustibly. The power structure can control if it will. It already has in such cities as Atlanta and Nashville, but its impact must be felt throughout the South. Thus and only thus can the dream of such Southerners as Graves and Faulkner, the dream of the realization of decency from within, come true.

Far better it is for the image of the South in the eyes of the world that it be taken in hand by its own leaders and led into reality rather than be hooked and gaffed by federal bayonets until it comes flopping, floundering in like a helpless trout.

As this survey shows, the desire is there. In the ultimate analysis, however, the voice of the moderate and enlightened power structure must be heard far more emphatically in the future than it has been in the past if the image of the South as the land of the raucous corn pone Claghorn, the South of the bombed Birmingham churches, the South of the assassins of the dark byways of Meridian, Memphis, Selma, and the lonely Georgia roads is to be changed into the South of Thomas Jefferson: "We hold these truths to be self-evident: that all men are created equal . . ."

# BIBLIOGRAPHY

## BOOKS

Cash, W. J. *The Mind of the South*. New York: Alfred A. Knopf, Inc., 1941.

Clark, Thomas D. *The Emerging South*. New York: Oxford University Press, Inc., 1961.

Cotterill, R. S. "The Old South to the New." In *The Pursuit of Southern History*, edited by G. B. Tindall. Baton Rouge: Louisiana State University Press, 1964.

Dollard, John. *Caste and Class in a Southern Town*. Garden City, N.Y.: Doubleday and Company, Inc., 1957.

Grantham, D. W. *The Democratic South*. Athens: University of Georgia Press, 1963.

Graves, John Temple. *The Fighting South*. New York: G. P. Putnam's Sons, 1943.

Key, V. O., Jr. *Southern Politics*. New York: Alfred A. Knopf, Inc., 1949.

Lerche, Charles O. *The Uncertain South*. Chicago: Quadrangle Books, Inc., 1964.

McGill, Ralph. *The South and the Southerner*. Boston: Little, Brown and Company, 1963.

McKean, Keith F. *Cross Currents in the South*. Denver: Alan Swallow, Publisher, 1960.

Nicholls, W. H. *Southern Tradition and Regional Progress.* Chapel Hill: University of North Carolina Press, 1960.

Reddick, L. D. "The Negro as Southerner and American." In *The Southerner as American,* edited by Charles G. Sellers, Jr. Chapel Hill: University of North Carolina Press, 1960.

Sellers, Charles G., Jr. (ed.). *The Southerner as American.* Chapel Hill: University of North Carolina Press, 1960.

Sindler, Allan P. (ed.). *Change in the Contemporary South.* Durham: Duke University Press, 1963.

Skaggs, William H. *The Southern Oligarchy.* New York: The Devin-Adair Company, 1924.

Soukup, James R., Clifton McCleskey, and Harry Holloway. *Party and Factional Division in Texas.* Austin: University of Texas Press, 1964.

Williams, T. Harry. *Romance and Realism in Southern Politics.* Athens: University of Georgia Press, 1961.

NEWSPAPERS QUOTED

*Fort Worth Star-Telegram* (Evening), March 5, 1966.

*Louisville Times,* November 16, 1965.

*New York Times,* May 2, 1954; May 6, 1954; January 22, 1956; May 8, 1958; June 4, 1958; June 5, 1958; January 11, 1960; May 3, 1962; May 5, 1962; May 9, 1962; May 30, 1962; August 8, 1963; August 28, 1963; August 29, 1963; December 3, 1963; December 9, 1963; January 13, 1964.

NEWSPAPERS RESPONDING TO QUESTIONNAIRE

*Alabama:*

*Andalusia Star-News*
*Anniston Star*
Athens *Courier-Democrat*

Bay Minette *Baldwin Times*
*Birmingham Post-Herald*
*Birmingham News*
*Brewton Standard*
Carrollton *Pickens County Herald*
*Decatur Daily*
*Dothan Eagle*
*Enterprise Ledger*
Fairfield *Steel City Star*
*Florence Times*
*Florence Tri-Cities Daily*
*Fort Payne Times-Journal*
Haleyville *Daily Northwest Alabamian*
*Hartselle Enquirer*
*Huntsville Times*
Jackson *South Alabamian*
Monroeville *Monroe Journal*
Oneonta *Southern Democrat*
*Roanoke Leader*
*Selma Times Journal*
*Sylacauga News*
*Tallassee Tribune*
*Thomasville Times*
*Tuscaloosa News*

*Louisiana*:

*Alexandria Daily Town Talk*
*Bastrop Daily Enterprise*
*Baton Rouge Morning Advocate*
*Bogalusa Daily News*
*Colfax Chronicle*

*Coushatta Citizen*
*Crowley Daily Signal*
*Denham Springs News*
*Donaldsonville Chief*
*Eunice News*
*Houma Courier*
*Jennings Daily News*
*Lafayette Advertiser*
*Lake Charles American Press*
*Minden Press*
Morgan City *Daily Review*
New Iberia *Daily Iberian*
New Orleans *Times-Picayune*
New Roads *Pointe Coupee Banner*
*Shreveport Times*
St. Martinville *Teche News*
*Sulphur Star-Builder*
Thibodaux *Lafourche Comet-Press*

*Mississippi*:

*Amory Advertiser*
Brookhaven *Leader-Advertiser*
*Clarksdale Press Register*
Charleston *Mississippi Sun*
Columbus *Commercial Dispatch*
Fulton *Itawamba County Times*
Greenville *Delta Democrat Times*
*Greenwood Commonwealth*
Gulfport *Daily Herald*
*Hattiesburg American*
Hazelhurst *Copiah County Courier*

Jackson *Clarion-Ledger*
*Laurel Leader-Call*
*Magee Courier*
McComb *Enterprise-Journal*
Ripley *Southern Sentinel*
*Starkville Daily News*
*Tunica Times-Democrat*
*Daily Tupelo Journal*
*Tylertown Times*
*Vicksburg Evening Post*
Water Valley *North Mississippi Herald*
Waveland and Bay St. Louis *Sea Coast Echo*
*Winona Times*
*Yazoo City Herald*

# Some Aspects of the Far Right Wing in Texas Politics

GEORGE NORRIS GREEN

THE CAUSES OF RIGHT-WING growth in Texas and United States politics have been traced to psychological and social factors, national events, and problems of international affairs.

Psychological causes of political fanaticism have been attributed primarily to major initial frustrations in childhood, especially harsh discipline and lack of love. The prevalence of hate in politics suggests that the most important private motive is a repressed and powerful anger toward authority. Individuals, consciously or not, may view their father as the source of their troubles. They often channel their frustrations toward the political system or person, such as the President, that stands as a father symbol.[1]

[1] Harold D. Lasswell, *Psychopathology and Politics* (New York: The Viking Press, Inc., 1960), p. 75; Bruno Bettelheim, "Why Does a Man Become a Hater?" *Life*, 56 (February 7, 1964), 78.

For many of these people hatred is inflamed because they feel that life has passed them by. A common American assumption is that everybody can make a success in life. Bruno Bettelheim adds: "If we assume that we can all go to the top, it follows if we do not there must be something wrong with us. This is a very painful conclusion. It attacks the very roots of our self-respect and leaves us open to the developing of some degree of self-hatred. And because all hate is basically retaliatory—a backlash at a seemingly hostile world—we grow to hate others."[2]

Among the social factors, anti-Semitism is often a part of right-wing politics. Jewish people are particularly handy scapegoats for frustrations, given their historic attachment to banking and commerce, their resistence to assimilation, and their culture centered around a non-Christian faith.[3]

A predisposition toward political extremism is also related to population growth and social mobility. The nation's fastest growing region, the Southwest, is the heartland of the radical Right. Where the size and composition of the local population are relatively stable, it is far more difficult for the extreme Right to make political inroads. Though Houston and Dallas have grown substantially since 1940, their relative increase has been

[2] Bettelheim, "Why Does a Man Become a Hater?," p. 78.
[3] See Nathan Glazer, "The Study of Man, The Authoritarian Personality in Profile," *Commentary*, 9 (June, 1950), 573–583, for a summary of the works of the leading writers in this field; see also Otto Fenichel, "A Psychoanalytic Approach to Anti-Semitism," *Commentary*, 2 (July ,1946), 36–44.

less than that of several smaller cities, Midland, Amarillo, and Odessa. Right-wing politics have been more important in these latter cities than in Dallas and Houston. A majority of the rightists are newcomers to the community, and most come from rural and small-town backgrounds. Generally they are moderately prosperous and middle class but have only recently attained this level. Some are upper class, but very few are manual laborers.[4]

A large proportion of the right wingers have college degrees—almost always in such technical fields as business and accounting, engineering, the natural sciences, and medicine and dentistry. Very few have been educated in the social sciences, humanities, law, theology, and fine arts. The rightists believe this to be a high tribute to the effective brainwashing conducted in these latter divisions of the modern American university.[5]

Another determinant of extremism is the degree of flexibility of traditional community and state leadership. There is not much opportunity for political leadership if the traditional office holders are able to keep the confidence of a city or state undergoing sudden changes. But the absorption of qualified

[4] Murray Havens, "The Radical Right in the Southwest: Community Response to Shifting Socio-Economic Patterns," a paper delivered at the annual meeting of the American Political Science Association, Chicago, Illinois, September, 9–12, 1964.

[5] Ibid.; Seymour Martin Lipset, "The Sources of the Radical Right," in *The Radical Right*, ed. Daniel Bell (Garden City, N.Y.: Doubleday and Company, Inc., 1963), p. 437.

people, especially new residents, into the leadership structure is necessary to stave off political tensions in a rapidly growing city or state. For instance, an ambitious and idealistic dentist moved to Lubbock, Texas, in the late 1940's and achieved immediate professional success. But his attempts to play an active role as a campaign manager, a candidate for mayor, and a leader in philanthropic drives were stifled by the city's social and political hierarchy. Convinced of the rottenness of the system, he became an effective leader of the John Birch Society. His commitment to the Right was doubtless genuine, but certainly quite rapid. Local speculation is that the chairmanship of the United Fund or a committee assignment in the country club might have made him a member and defender of the city's Establishment. His experience has been repeated in several Texas towns where a small number of closely knit families have traditionally constituted the local power structure.[6]

The Establishment's rejection of economically advancing groups and individuals cannot always be traced to snobbery and clannishness. Only recently affluent, many of the new rich are unable to adjust to middle- and upper-class mores. Their rural background, fundamentalist religion, and relatively narrow education leave them ill-prepared for positions of leadership in modern urban America. The rightists are, in fact, repelled by a number of aspects of this urban culture—the place of women in the society and home; the changed patterns of

6 Havens, "The Radical Right in the Southwest."

sexual behavior, especially among young people; modern art, literature, and theater; mental health and water fluoridation; and progressive education.[7]

The fundamentalist churches, traditionally a powerful force in the South and in Texas, have also been caught up in right-wing politics. Opposition to liberalism, especially in regard to the social gospel, unites the religious zealots with the political extremists. The conflict with communism is not one of power blocs but of faiths, part of the ancient and unending struggle between God and the devil. The danger of communism is from within, from the corrosion of faith by the insidious doctrines of socialism or collectivism—the modern fundamentalist's secular counterpart of atheism. Some fundamentalists join the racists and the political extremists in attacking the recent Supreme Court decisions upholding the separation of church and state. Rooting Communists out of the public schools is a particular concern in Texas, where a group of mostly fundamentalist businessmen once offered $10,000 to any Texas school that would teach "Americanism" from the group's material.[8]

National factors promoting right wing politics include the depression of the 1930's, which evoked social and economic reforms that undermined conservative and business predomi-

[7] Ibid.

[8] Betty Chmaj, "Paranoid Patriotism: The Radical Right and the South," *Atlantic Monthly*, 210 (November, 1962), 93; David Danzig, "The Radical Right and the Rise of the Fundamentalist Minority," *Commentary*, 33 (April, 1962), 292.

nance in the nation. Since World War II most conservatives have come to accept the various New Deal reforms and to tolerate the labor movement, but the radical Right still opposes such welfare state measures as social security and the Tennessee Valley Authority. And they despise the government-sponsored gains made by organized labor in the 1930's, such as the Wagner Act, which guaranteed collective bargaining, and the Fair Labor Standards Act, which established minimum wages and maximum hours. The rightists (as well as plain reactionaries) want the federal government to cease such interference in the workings of the American economy and to return to its policies of the 1920's and earlier, when the government refused to intervene in the economy except to aid big business.[9]

To explain the calamities of the New Deal the rightists often attribute them to Communist penetration. The idea of Communist subversion, to the far right wing, extends beyond the notion that a few New Dealers were overly sympathetic to communism and that several Communists held government posts. They believe there has been a sustained conspiracy among American leaders since the advent of Franklin Roosevelt, that all the top branches of the government have been infiltrated by Communists since the 1930's, and that the nation is filled with Communist agents. This conspiratorial out-

[9] Richard Hofstadter, "Pseudo-Conservatism Revisited: A Postscript," in *The Radical Right*, ed. Bell, p. 103; Lipset, "Sources of the Radical Right," pp. 332–333.

look is hardly new in America. It was found among the Antimasons, Know-Nothings, Greenbackers, Populists, anti-munitions propagandists of the 1920's and 1930's, and the popular left-wing press of the 1930's, as well as among the contemporary Right. Such charges of subversion may in part be merely a recent expression of Populist-type extremism against the eastern upper class. The old seaboard aristocracy has traditionally dominated governmental and intellectual public opinion and the Foreign Service, excluding such main-stays of the far Right as Midwestern isolationists and newly rich Texans. The old Populist and Bob La Follette phrase, "internationalist, Anglophile snob," has been replaced by "egghead security risk," according to some theorists.[10]

Ethnic prejudice, particularly in the South and the South-west, has played a role in the expansion of the far right wing. The Supreme Court's advocacy of school integration in the Brown case of 1954 revived the Ku Klux Klan and gave birth to the White Citizens' Councils. By 1957 it was standard for the extremists to equate the Supreme Court, the National Association for the Advancement Colored People, and the Communist party, all dedicated to the overthrow of "normal" race relations. This prejudice against civil rights for Negroes in-volved more than the maintenance of long-time traditions; it

[10] Richard Hofstadter, "The Paranoid Style in American Politics," *Harper's Magazine*, 229 (November, 1964), 78, 81–82; Seymour Martin Lipset, *Political Man* (Garden City, N.Y.: Doubleday and Company, Inc., 1960), pp. 170–171; Peter Viereck, "The Revolt against the Elite," in *The Radical Right*, ed. Bell, p. 172.

was also based upon the economic threat presented by Negro workers and businessmen, desire of the white employers to maintain a cheap labor supply, and housewives' fear of losing their cheap and docile domestic help. By 1961 the racists had linked up with some military establishments in the South and Southwest that were educating and propagandizing their troops with anti-Communist literature and promoting joint civil-military seminars to expose communism. These two forces of reaction had discovered that international communism was their common enemy and that the Communist–Supreme Court–NAACP conspiracy was bent on destroying the South, our largest region and primary military bastion. Some Southerners seemed entranced with notions of "victory" and "struggle to the death." There were always military officers attending the anti-Communist rallies, if only to sit in uniform on the platform. The racists also allied with state and local law enforcement agencies. The Southern Association of Intelligence Agents was established in 1961 to offer its services to the Federal Bureau of Investigation in tracking down subversives.[11]

International events, especially since World War II, have

[11] Chmaj, "Paranoid Patriotism," pp. 91–92; Wilma Dykeman and James Stokely, "The Klan Tries a Comeback," *Commentary*, 29 (January, 1960), 47; Alan Barth, "Report on the Rampageous Right," *New York Times Magazine*, November 26, 1961, p. 25; Victor Bernstein, "The Anti-Labor Front," *Antioch Review*, 3 (Fall, 1943), 336, 338; Mike Newberry, *The Yahoos* (New York: Marzani and Munsell, 1964), pp. 30–32.

contributed to the rise of the right wing. For the first time in American history, the nation consciously accepts leadership in international affairs, lives with the possibility of physical destruction, and contains a public that declares a high concern for foreign policy in peacetime, even though most Americans are still unskilled in interpreting international relations. After it became apparent that the Republican administration of Dwight Eisenhower was not going to end what many Americans regarded as the appeasement of the Soviet Union, extremists in the late 1950's and early 1960's tapped the public alarm over Berlin, bomb shelters, the Congo, and Laos. There was no clear-cut American victory in a number of these crises, a new experience for Americans accustomed to dramatic triumphs in warfare. The far right wing, growing in numbers and in wealth, called for a war to the death with the Soviets.[12]

It is essential to define what is meant in this treatise by the term "right wing" and by those phrases used as synonyms, "radical Right," "extreme Right," "far Right," and "rightist." These terms apply to individuals and groups who defy both the wisdom and the legitimacy of numerous public policies now in effect and who tend to challenge the validity of the constitutional structure. Their alienation must be based on a cohesive ideology or at least on opposition to several particular

[12] Alan Westin, "The Deadly Parallels, Radical Right and Radical Left," *Harper's Magazine*, 224 (April, 1962), 26–27, 31; Arnold Forster and Benjamin Epstein, *Danger on the Right* (New York: Random House, Inc., 1964), p. 6.

policies or values. Rightist beliefs may or may not violate norms or laws; the question is whether they can be reconciled with the system as it presently operates. The Constitution provides for the impeachment of the chief justice of the Supreme Court, for instance, but only for high crimes and misdemeanors, not, as the rightists desire, for mistakes in policy. Moreover, the style in which ideas are presented, as in an outburst of conspiratorial fantasy, may be more important than their truth or falsity.[13]

Eric Hoffer describes the primary requirements for extremist leadership:

. . . audacity and a joy in defiance; an iron will; a fanatical conviction that he is in possession of the one and only truth; faith in his destiny and luck; a capacity for passionate hatred; contempt for the present; a cunning estimate of human nature; a delight in symbols (spectacles and ceremonials); unbounded brazenness which finds expression in a disregard of consistence and fairness; a recognition that the innermost craving of a following is for communion . . . ; a capacity for winning and holding the loyalty of a group of able lieutenants.[14]

The right wing is overwhelmingly authoritarian—that is, generally intolerant of ambiguity, approving of strong leadership, and favoring harsh punishment for violators of social

---

[13] Havens, "The Radical Right in the Southwest."

[14] Eric Hoffer, *The True Believer: Thoughts on the Nature of Mass Movements* (New York: The New American Library, Inc., 1963), pp. 105–106.

norms. Rightist beliefs and values could only be impressed upon the United States by strong government, yet most of the intellectual and political spokesmen of the far Right proclaim a belief in libertarianism, complete liberty for all. But even though most rightists are theoretically committed to individualism, only a few are such consistent, thoroughgoing individualists that they extend this doctrine to its logical conclusion, philosophical anarchy.[15]

Many extremist groups, programs, and publications sprang up in Texas in the 1950's and 1960's—notably Facts and Forum and Life Line, propaganda outlets for oil billionaire H. L. Hunt; the Minute Women, whose Houston branch was singularly effective in cleansing the city's schools of political liberalism; the Dan Smoot Report, put out by a former FBI man in Dallas; the National Indignation Convention, which arose overnight in Dallas to protest Yugoslavian pilots on American soil, especially Texas soil; and finally the John Birch Society. None of these organizations proved as effective in a one-shot effort as J. Evetts Haley and the outfit he spearheaded, Texans for America (many of whom were Birchers and Minute Women). Textbooks were their targets.

Texas schools buy from $6 million to $10 million worth

[15] Lipset, "Sources of the Radical Right," pp. 359–360; idem, "Three Decades of the Radical Right," in *The Radical Right*, ed. Bell, pp. 411–414, 420; Clinton Rossiter, *Conservatism in America* (New York: Random House, Inc., 1962), pp. 166–170. See also Ralph Ellsworth and Sarah Harris, *The American Right Wing* (Washington, D. C.: Public Affairs Press, 1962), pp. 11–12.

of textbooks a year. The State Textbook Committee selects five books for each public-school course, from which local boards choose any one. For the benefit of the committee, Haley expounded his criteria for evaluating the texts: "The stressing of both sides of a controversy only confuses the young and encourages them to make snap judgments based on insufficient evidence. Until they are old enough to understand both sides of a question, they should be taught only the American side."[16]

Haley rallied the Daughters of the American Revolution, several American Legion posts, and various John Birchers in dominating the State Textbook Committee hearings in the early 1960's. He avowed that two hundred Texans were working with him. They were assisted with propaganda from rightist groups all over the nation.[17]

Generally the Haleyites proposed deleting from all textbooks any favorable mention of the income tax, social security, TVA, federal subsidies to farmers and schools, the United Nations, disarmament, integration, and the Supreme Court. Among those Haley listed as subversive tools of the Communists and internationalists were Albert Schweitzer, John Gunther, Stephen Vincent Benét, Ralph Bunche, and Langston Hughes. After a publisher replied that Hughes was an internationally known Negro poet and winner of several awards, among them the Guggenheim Fellowship for Creative

[16] Jack Nelson and Gene Roberts, *The Censors and the Schools* (Boston: Little, Brown and Company, 1963), pp. 120–121.
[17] Ibid., pp. 121–122.

Writing, Haley declared that this only demonstrated the degenerate nature of the people who decided the awards. Southern Methodist University history professor Paul Boller, who had stated that the Communist party is practically defunct in this country, was accused by Haley of being "soft on Communism, short on logic, or both." Boller's publisher, Webster Company, was labeled a Communist collaborationist for publishing a government-contracted pamphlet about the Soviet Union that was circulated among the armed forces during World War II.[18]

Typical of Haley's group was R. A. Kilpatrick, a lawyer from Cleburne. He objected to one textbook's listing of Upton Sinclair, Jack London, Ida Tarbell, and Lincoln Steffens as novelists who wrote of the evils around them. Kilpatrick said this was promoting the writings of known subversives, especially since there were pictures of London and Steffens in the book. He also noticed that there was only one mention of Will Rogers and that, at the end of the chapter, the student was not asked to gather additional material on him. The lawyer concluded, "Guess he was too American for the author of this textbook!"[19]

---

[18] Ibid., pp. 122, 123, 126; *Dallas Morning News*, October 6, 1960, and September 16, 1961; Willie Morris, "Cell 772, or Life among the Extremists," *Commentary*, 38 (October, 1964), 37–38.

[19] Nelson and Roberts, *Censors and the Schools*, pp. 123–124. Haleyites at various times also charged that a history text picture of George Washington, done by a contemporary of the president, "looks as if George Gobel posed for the painting," that the song, "He's Got

The State Textbook Committee made frightening concessions to the censors. In October, 1961, the committee approved fifty books for adoption, including twenty-seven the Texans for America had condemned. But the committee had rejected twelve books opposed by this group and had ordered some changes in every book approved. Many other alterations are not reflected in the Texas Education Agency records because they were agreed to orally in secret sessions between publishers and the committee. All references to and works by Pete Seeger and Langston Hughes were ordered deleted from Texas schoolbooks because of connections with groups cited by the House Un-American Activities Committee. All mention of Vera Micheles Dean had to be omitted from Ginn and Company's *American History* for a similar reason. Laidlaw Brothers had to drop its reference to Dorothy Canfield Fisher and others. Macmillan's text, *History of a Free People*, had to take a more positive stand against communism. It had to delete the passage, "Had Wilson seen the necessity for compromise, the United States would have joined the League, although with reservations. Had that happened, there was just a chance that World War II might have been averted."[20]

The Silver Burdett Company was forced to make numerous

the Whole World in His Hands," smacked of one-worldism, and that Mohammed's quote, "Trust in God, but tie your camel," was dangerous because Mohammed was not a true prophet (ibid., p. 125; *Texas Observer*, November 18, 1960).

[20] *Dallas Morning News*, October 6, 1961; Nelson and Roberts, *Censors and the Schools*, pp. 127–130.

modifications in its geography text. Among the alterations, which indicate how the character of a book can be changed by censorship, were:

Original version: "Because it needs to trade, and because it needs military help, the United States needs the friendship of countries throughout the world. But, to keep its friends, a country must help them too." Changed to: "The United States trades with countries in all parts of the world. We are also providing military help to many nations. In addition, the United States helps many countries in other ways."[21]

Even after making substantial modifications, publishers and authors discovered that many local school officials were unwilling to buy a book that had been under attack. D. C. Heath and Company estimated that their high school history book sales were $80,000 below what sales records had led them to anticipate. Paul Boller contended that sales for his book were considerably reduced by the Haleyite attacks.[22]

Moreover, Haley's crusade launched a right-wing onslaught onto the Texas public schools. The superpatriots in the towns and cities were inspired to weed out "communism"—that is, liberalism and the free exchange of ideas. In parts of West Texas the textbook battles fomented a purge of library shelves. At Amarillo's four high schools and at Amarillo College, John Birchers directed the removal from the shelves of ten

21 Nelson and Roberts, *Censors and the Schools*, p. 130.
22 Ibid., pp. 126, 132.

novels, including four Pulitzer Prize winners. Listed as subversive or Communist and withdrawn from circulation were
such works as *Andersonville, Brave New World, Marjorie
Morningstar, The Big Sky, Grapes of Wrath,* and *1984.* It is
ironic that *1984* was purged, since the book is usually regarded
as a devastating critique of life under communism. Some of
the same volumes were purged from school libraries in Midland, where Harold Hitt, chairman of the State Textbook
Committee, was superintendent of schools. Texans for America circulated a pamphlet declaring that forty-two books at
the high school library had been randomly examined and that
the same ten novels removed in Amarillo had been judged
totally unfit for consumption at any age level. Political over-
tones were absent from many of the censored books, but their
alleged obscenity was considered part of the Communist conspiracy to undermine America's morals and conquer from
within.[23]

Dr. William D. Kelley, an associate of Haley in the
textbook hearings, was a member of the Midland school
board. An anonymous letter was sent out to many Midland
teachers asking them to evaluate their principals and administrations, with instructions to return their answers to Kelley.
Kelley denied knowing anything about it. Midland was also

[23] Ibid., pp. 132–133; *Texas Observer,* November 16, 1962; Murray
Havens, "The Impact of Right Wing Groups in Selected Texas
Cities," unpublished article, 1963, personal possession of Professor
Havens; Forster and Epstein, *Danger on the Right,* p. 4.

the scene of the attempted expulsion from school of a seven-teen-year-old high school senior for his "subversive" remarks in a speech—he had quoted *Time* magazine's opinion of the John Birch Society. At Dumas, another West Texas site, the public schools were subjected to a program of compulsory patriotism. The school board, consisting of a rancher, a drug-gist, a lawyer, and two oil company executives, made sure the curricula included lessons in religious fundamentalism and poiltical ultraconservatism.[24]

The flames of rightist extremism in Houston schools were also fanned by the textbook hearings. Houston, however, al-ready had a heritage of extremism in its school system. The Minute Women, organized nationwide from Connecticut in 1949, constituted the most powerful pressure group in Hous-ton since the heyday of the Ku Klux Klan in the 1920's. In order to prevent being taken over by the Communists, the Houston chapter, like all local branches, held no elections and had no bylaws or constitution. All appointments and laws were handled by the president of the group in Connecticut, Mrs. Suzanne Silvercruys Stevenson. Drawing much of their strength from the exclusive River Oaks section in Houston, the Minute Women reached their peak in 1952 with a little over five hundred members. Well over a hundred of the ladies were

24 *Texas Observer*, November 16, 1962; Anti-Defamation League Files, *William D. Kelley Folder*, Regan Legg, Midland attorney, "Re-port on William D. Kelley;" Tristram Coffin, "The New Know-Nothings," *Progressive*, 25 (December, 1961), 11.

wives of physicians and oil industry personnel. This group purged textbooks of information about the "Communistic" United Nations, stifled free speech with mass heckling of a Quaker meeting in 1952 (accusing the Quakers of subversion), induced the Houston Chamber of Commerce and the Texas State Teachers Association to abandon three of their proposed speakers, forced the banning of the annual United Nations examination contest through which students could win college scholarships and trips abroad, and prevented the school board from hiring George Ebey as assistant superintendent because he was an integrationist and was not a "militant combatant of Communism."[25]

By 1961 Houston was probably the only place in the country where the Minute Women still functioned, at least as an action group. One of these ladies heard that Kenneth Parker, a young history teacher, had dropped a few controversial comments in class. To check for herself she asked him to her home, played a tape recording of a superpatriotic speech, and quizzed Parker on his opinions. Still dissatisfied, she persuaded the school board president to check on him formally. She allegedly received special reports from adults who came into Parker's classes and took notes. After a long controversy, he resigned, reporting in exasperation that he was a Christian and a Kennedy Democrat. The Minute Woman believed his de-

[25] "The Facts," June–July, 1952; Ralph O'Leary, columns in the *Houston Post*, October 11–12, 1953; *Houston Chronicle*, January 30, 1952.

parture was a good thing "because of his reluctance to tell he
was a Christian and the ultraliberal views he expounded in the
classroom."[26]

The Houston school board was still dominated by patrioteers. The president of the board, a member of the Daughters of the American Revolution, had won the Houston Sons
of the Revolution's award for her "continuing battle against
socialistic liberalism in modern education." She was also successful in rejecting federal funds for milk for school children.
She spearheaded the board's refusal to allow the American
Civil Liberties Union to rent one of the school auditoriums,
because its thinking "was not in keeping with that of Hous-
tonians." Soon thereafter the board announced that two
loyalty oaths would be required for future rentals, one by an
officer of the group involved and one by the proposed speaker.
"We don't want any Communist speakers or Communist
group meetings in our public schools," the president said.[27]
But it was all right for right-wing extremists. At Jesse Jones
High School, for instance, students attended weekly anticom-
munism programs and saw such films as *Operation Abolition*
and others from the radical right-wing Harding College in
Searcy, Arkansas.[28]

Higher education also fell prey to the rightist outburst of

[26] Willie Morris, "Houston's Superpatriots," *Harper's Magazine*,
223 (October, 1961), 54.
[27] Ibid.
[28] Ibid., pp. 52–53.

1961–1962. One of several extremist invasions occurred in Odessa in the spring of 1961. Two Odessa Junior College instructors, Dick Harley and James Dickson, were invited to participate in a "debate" on the local television station. They were supposed to favor Medicare; their opponents, an attorney and a physician, were to speak against it. The attorney and the doctor, neither of whom could even define "socialism," accused the teachers of being sympathetic with socialism and communism. Irate, middle-of-the-night telephone calls rousted the regents out of their beds. The instructors were quizzed by the regents. Three superpatriots declared as write-in candidates for the regents' positions. One of them noted that all college personnel were "employees of the taxpayers" and could go elsewhere if they did not want to conform to the standards of Americanism. The movement collapsed, but only at the very high cost of the teachers' having publicly to pledge their undying loyalty to the free enterprise system for having dared to argue in favor of (without endorsing) President Kennedy's plan for medical care for the aged.[29]

The textbook battles also sparked a legislative investigation of communism in the schools, an action inspired by Mrs. A. A. Forrester, the DAR's leading book censor in Texas and a strong Haley supporter. In 1961 the Texas house established a five-man committee to look into the content of schoolbooks.

[29] *Odessa American*, March 12 and 19, 1961; transcript of KOSA-TV (Odessa) program, March 16, 1961; interview with Dick Harley, Arlington, Texas, September 19, 1966.

The chairman of the committee was W. T. Dungan of Mc-Kinney, best known for his introduction of a bill to require every public school, college, and university teacher in Texas to swear his belief in a Supreme Being.[30]

Dungan allowed the textbook censors to delve into a variety of subjects—mental health, fluoridation, alleged obscenities, and the socialistic trend since the turn of the century. Many of the patrioteers began their testimony by divulging that although they had read no textbooks, they knew just the same that communism pervaded the public schools. Typical was the Reverend R. D. Wade of the Trinity Baptist Church in Austin. He said he had not read any texts but had been offended by a television show on which two theologians had laughed at the John Birch Society's belief that there were Communists in the White House. He had "no doubt" that there were Communists in the White House but confided that he was too busy winning souls for Christ to "document" his charge.[31]

During the hearings in Amarillo, the legislators entertained twenty-three censors who had no opposition and who frequently asked questions as well as testified. When liberal Representative Ronald Roberts was away from the hearing room briefly, one witness, Mrs. Harold Boots, exclaimed, "Well, what happened to the gentleman from Hillsboro? I had a question for him. I wanted to ask him how long he had been a card-carrying Communist." Heavy applause followed.

[30] Nelson and Roberts, *Censors and the Schools*, pp. 134–136.
[31] Ibid., pp. 135–136.

Roberts, who sued the lady for $85,000, received a letter from Governor Price Daniel expressing his shock at the slanderous attack. Mrs. Boots also told Representative John Alaniz that he had no business on the committee because he was a Catholic, and she alleged that one elementary school text was "full of Catholic propaganda."[32]

By late May, 1962, the committee members themselves had second thoughts about the value of the flamboyant meetings. Only chairman Dungan showed up for the Dallas hearings. Since there was no quorum, Dungan admitted the meeting might not be official, but went ahead with it anyway. Witness W. T. White, superintendent of the Dallas schools, defended the present methods of textbook selection but quickly added that Dallas teachers were more conservative than the average citizen. J. Evetts Haley took the stand again and disagreed with Dr. White, "who is in charge of these premises only temporarily," that the selection of textbooks was a professional matter. "Free enterprise," Haley said, "offers a better method of education than socialized education." He also called for an investigation of publishing companies. General Edwin A. Walker testified that all morality was based on Christianity, and that this system was being undermined by psychiatrists, psychologists, and social workers through a "military con-

[32] Ibid., pp. 141–142. Mrs. Boots later claimed her charge against Roberts was made under immunity because she was testifying before a legislative committee. Roberts disagreed, but dropped his suit in light of the Supreme Court's Sullivan decision, which allows considerable leeway in charges against public figures.

spiracy with communism." A twelve-year-old junior high student condemned a history text for not mentioning Christianity and added, "We'll never get peace until the Second Coming of Christ. They talk about world peace in there and I'm not in favor of that."[33]

At its next meeting the textbook investigating committee ruled that the Dallas meeting was illegal and denied Dungan state funds to pay for it. The state did pay for eight hundred copies of the Dallas testimony, which Dungan was caught selling for his personal profit in 1963. Each copy bore a concluding statement from Dungan that various history and economics books in the public schools ought to be removed. Also, during the 1963 legislative session, Dungan introduced a bill to require all Texas high schools to teach a course in "capitalism vs. communism," stressing the superiority of the former. The man from McKinney noted that he was concerned about the inroads of socialism into our free enterprise system. There was, however, no legislative enactment on textbook censorship or the proposed course.[34]

Yet the fiery crusade launched by Haley, brief as it was, could claim a partial victory. Textbooks had been altered and dropped. An atmosphere of fanaticism enveloped the supposedly dispassionate sittings of textbook committee and legislative hearings. The loyalty of college professors was questioned. The school systems of Amarillo, Midland, Dumas, and

[33] *Texas Observer*, June 8, 1962.
[34] Ibid., March 21, 1963.

Houston were infected with rightist sentiment, and other school systems were probably inspired by their example. In 1964 Elden Busby, superintendent of schools in Fort Worth, wrote that his schools emphasized the superiority of Americans and private enterprise and the evils of communism, socialism, and fascism, from the first through the twelfth grades. Each Fort Worth teacher had to sign an oath that he had never been a subversive and would always defend the Texas and United States constitutions. In addition, Dr. Busby noted that "each teacher personally exemplifies the qualities of Americanism and good citizenship so important to his pupils."[35]

It is on the local level that the rightists are an established threat, both in running for mayoralties, city councils, and school boards and in arousing pressures to influence these officials. It is easier for the extremists to get together on one or two local issues than on more complex state matters. A well-financed state race also costs prohibitively. In addition, many members of the far Right have been relatively unknown. Rightist attempts for nonlocal offices in the 1930's and 1940's were almost total failures, and there were not many more successes in the 1950's and 1960's. Pressuring local officials to bend to the right has doubtless been the most consistently successful tactic. High schools and small colleges in particular are too often served by parochial, undistinguished, and easily swayed regents and boards.

[35] Ibid., June 26, 1964.

The far right wing, of course, is a national phenomenon. Psychological deprivations, rapid changes in society and in basic laws, and the perils of the struggle with communism are burdens shared by all Americans. But Texas is widely considered the heartland of the far Right, and not without reason.

One distinguishing characteristic that promotes Texas extremism is what might be called Texanism or Super-Americanism. Americans have enjoyed a history of security and success that has made us conscious of our strength and superiority. This history has given us what Sir Denis Brogan calls "the illusion of American omnipotence." The illusion is magnified in Texas, the only state that ever really stood as a viable republic and long the biggest state in the Union (some say it still is—wait till Alaska melts). Of all the states, only Texas won her own independence by shedding her own blood on her own soil and hurling back a "foreign invader." The conformity and lack of self-criticism in Texanism is different from the pride of a Bostonian in Boston or of a Californian in California. Texans believe that there is a political difference between their state and other states and that the federal government is almost a foreign menace to Texas rights and privileges. Texas history is treated in the public schools as if it were about as important as United States history. State law even allows college students to substitute three hours of Texas history for one-half the required six hours of American history. The state's history and legends and heroes are taught to its children with far greater intensity than a Boston child is taught of the Battle of Bunker Hill. Not many years ago the Texas constitution, a documental derelict in the twentieth century, was defended against revisionists on the grounds of being sacred.[36]

Theodore White, writing in the 1950's, held that Texanism was a form of nationalism that began as more or less a joke, "as simple braggadocio about the biggest state with the prettiest girls and the fightingest men in the Union." If so, the humor was lost before the era described herein. Writing in the 1940's, John Gunther declared that no other state was so lacking in wholesome self-criticism and that no other state could equal Texas' nationalism.[37]

Another Texas trait that seems to promote extremism is that it is a one-party state with two powerful, organized factions. The one-party situation, in which government and politics seem to be frozen at some paleolithic stage of evolution, is the state's heritage from the South and the Civil War. With only one party, considerable dissidence is inevitable within it—there is no other place to go. Despite bitter warfare, the Democrats find themselves in the same ring when the struggle is over. The frustrations and frayed nerves that arise produce political hatreds that few states can surpass. What other state can boast of a governor (Connally) and a senator

[36] Theodore White, "Texas: Land of Wealth and Fear," *Reporter*, 10 (June 8, 1954), 35; Louis J. Halle, "What's Eating Us?" *New Republic*, 151 (September 19, 1964), 19.

[37] White, "Texas," p. 35; John Gunther, *Inside U.S.A.* (New York: Harper and Brothers, Publishers, 1947), pp. 815–822.

(Yarborough) in the same party who did not like to speak to each other and who took every opportunity to undermine each other for six years? Other states have one-party systems, but Texas is much richer than any of them; the vested interests and their opponents have more to win or lose here.[38]

Another facet of extremism in Texas is that it is the only state where Southern, Western, and Mexican traditions meet. Although this amalgam produces a cosmopolitanism unusual in the South and Southwest, it does not always operate for the public good. The 1,500,000 to 2,000,000 Mexican-Americans live in ignorance and political inertia. They are more poorly educated, have a lower income, and are probably more culturally isolated than Texas Negroes. Many of them are manipulated by unscrupulous political bosses who are contemptuous of the democratic process and who will make deals with anyone who suits their purposes; this is a rather slothful brand of local extremist rule. A more active ingredient in promoting state-wide extremism is the Old South legacy of ignorance, illiteracy, fundamentalism, States' rights at all costs, and a streak of violence. Perhaps the area's rightist thought is best summarized by a man writing from Denison, "There are two things that every genuine, true American should have at his fingertips at all times: a gun and a Bible."[39]

[38] Gunther, *Inside U.S.A.*, pp. 845–846.

[39] Lonnie Roberts, letter to the *Dallas Morning News*, March 19, 1966. Texas, incidentally, ranks eleventh in illiteracy, and all save one of the states with higher rates are Southern (*Austin American-*

As for the Western heritage, logrollings, the building of forts, and other socialistic endeavors have been cited to demonstrate that the idea of the frontier as a haven for individualism is a myth. This thesis may be correct, but West Texans are individualistic, sometimes to the point of anarchy, and they think it is a frontier heritage. Frontier individualism may be a historical myth, but it is being lived as a present-day fact. West Texas extremist politics are couched in frontier rhetoric. As the right wing Midland dentist, William Kelley, wrote in support of General Walker, ". . . if our grandfathers had fought the Indians and Red Coats like we are fighting the Communists, we wouldn't be alive today." West Texas and the West-Central Texas hill country are arid, sparse regions with extremes of heat and cold, droughts and floods, and ragged peaks. Such an environment, bound to leave an imprint on its people, has helped produce a lonely, suspicious citizenry, slow to change. The environment and the frontier and vigilante memories seem to help spawn a certain amount of political extremism.

Texas extremism, as noted with the general origins of this radicalism, also feeds upon the enormous changes in the state in the past thirty years. A generation ago cotton was still king; the 16 million acres once devoted to it have now shrunk to 6 million. Odessa claimed only about 2,400 people in 1930;

Statesman, June 13, 1964). See also Sheldon Hackney, "Southern Violence," American Historical Review, 74 (February, 1969), 906–925.

today it has over 80,000. In the same period Houston climbed
from about 290,000 to over a million. It boasts that in each
year but one since World War II it has led the nation's cities
in construction and capital investment. In 1930 Dallas was a
wholesaling and cotton-trading center. Today it is the financial
capital of the Southwest, with two of the nation's top twenty-
five banks and a host of insurance companies. In the 1930's
and on into the 1940's many of the newly urban rich who
financed the far Right, such as Hugh Roy Cullen, Sid Richard-
son, Clint Murchison, and H. L. Hunt (later the most active
and farthest to the right), were preoccupied with making their
first 10 or 20 million dollars. As one millionaire phrased it
in the 1950's: "We all made money fast. We were interested
in nothing else. Then this Communist business burst upon us.
Were we going to lose what we had gained?"[40]

Fear of economic loss actually haunts the millionaires less
acutely than it does the business and professional people who
make up the bulk of the extremists. The economic power of
these Texas extremists gives political meaning to their reaction against social change. As Theodore White wrote:

These elements—the common national struggle, the unsettling
effect of rapid change, the myths of Texanism—are in themselves
almost enough to explain why Texas politics has taken on such
a peculiar cast. But when all these elements are manipulated by

[40] Charles J. V. Murphy, "Texas Business and McCarthy," *Fortune*,
49 (May, 1954), 101; White, "Texas," p. 34; *Texas Almanac*, 1966,
pp. 133–138.

clever men and by the kind of money the Little Rich—the prosperous car dealers, the contractors, the bottling concessionaires, the little oil men, the real estate men—can make available to state candidates of their choice, these emotions can be made to stand up and march.[41]

Some of the blame for political tension must inevitably be attached to the mass media. And surely no state in the Union has a more monolithically reactionary press than Texas. Some newspapers are openly extremist, like the *Borger News-Herald*, the *Houston Tribune*, R. C. Hoiles' *Odessa American*, and his three Valley papers. But even the supposedly respectable family press, led by the *Dallas Morning News*, has given the far Right a creditable platform from which to crusade against the liberalist-socialist-communist-atheist infidel. The *News*, for instance, considers the presidency of Franklin Roosevelt as actually destructive of the Republic, the Senate's censure of Joe McCarthy as "a happy day for Communists," and the Supreme Court as "a threat to state sovereignty second only to Communism itself." When they take a stand on anything, radio and television stations echo this ultraconservative drumbeat of conformity. The effects of the mass media upon deeds and votes cannot readily be measured, but as was noted long ago, "Whatsoever a man soweth, that shall he also reap."[42]

Extremism seems more virulent in Texas than in the other

41 White, "Texas," p. 35.

42 Ibid., pp. 34–35; George Fuermann, *Reluctant Empire* (Garden City, N.Y.: Doubleday and Company, Inc., 1957), p. 130; "Tussle in Texas," *Nation*, 198 (February 3, 1964), 115.

two notable areas of its existence, Southern California and
Florida. Neither of these states has anything approaching
Texas' nationalism (nor do any other states except perhaps
Virginia and New England as a region). While California has
a two-party system, Florida has the same one-party machinery
as Texas. But Florida's Democratic party does not contain two
powerful, organized interest groups. Indeed, Florida politics
are among the most diffused and open in the nation. As for
the three cultural heritages, California lacks the Southern and
Florida lacks the Western and Mexican. All three states have
undergone tremendous and rapid social change. California's
extremist wealth probably equals that of Texas, but Florida's
does not. California's mass media probably match those of
Texas in emotional tone and strength of conviction, but California publications range over the entire political spectrum.
Florida's press is more like Texas' in the uniformity of conservatism. But the Texas press seems more militant than Florida's and contains no more than one moderately liberal daily,
compared with at least three major ones in the smaller state
of Florida.

The radical Right in Texas seems to have declined in power
since 1962. Contributing factors were repeated defeats at the
polls, the tactically unwise scattered and simultaneous attacks
on schools, city governments, and churches, and, perhaps,
the assassination of President Kennedy on Texas soil. Pub-
licity, some of it adverse, about the Minute Women, the
Birchers, and Texans for America may have hindered their

effectiveness in some instances. But the appeal of the far Right is still very much present. There is no reason to believe that any of its general causes—psychological and social factors, national events, and international affairs—will decrease or be handled differently in any manner that would lessen right-wing fervor.

Although Texas rightists are still active in the late 1960's, they attract less support and fewer headlines than during the early years of the decade. They most recently rallied for George Wallace, in his futile 1968 race for the presidency. Wallace received over 20 percent of the Texas vote, but a number of his followers probably could not be classified as right-wing extremists. Many were apparently stirred only by a racist appeal, which cannot stand alone as a determinant of extremism. The easiest way of maintaining contact with the rightists in this relatively quiescent period is to dial Let Freedom Ring. The Dallas (LA 2-1360) and Fort Worth (WA 7-8764) branches offer two different weekly messages. When this writer dialed the Fort Worth center the second week of April, 1969, the recording charged that the United States is paying for an all-weather highway being constructed between the Soviet Union and Southeast Asia.

To help prevent these rightists from enjoying a rebirth of influence, moderate-minded Texans ought to make a more concerted effort to fill legislative posts with learned men— men who would not vote to repeal the income tax or to investgate ordinary textbooks for alleged Communist sympathies. A two-party system is also desirable. With the help of court-ordered reapportionment the Republican party made the beginnings of a comeback in the fall elections of 1966. Whether a two-party system is really wanted if one of the parties, particularly in West Texas, is influenced by Birchers is a moot question. As the Texas Republicans capture three or four congressional seats and a dozen legislative posts, however, they will be lured by the desire to grow still more; to do that they will have to moderate their right-wing stance in the long run.

Outside the strictly political realm, business leaders need to launch a clear ideological counterattack to separate free enterprise from the nihilistic propositions of the far Right and to educate careless corporation executives against financial support and verbal endorsement of extremist activities. Business organizations must become more aware of the dangers created by many of the alarmist anti-Communist speeches from the radical Right. These speeches may start by denouncing Moscow or Peking, but they usually wind up as campaigns to fire a town librarian who has pro-Communist books on the shelf or to prevent an art gallery from hanging a Picasso painting.[43] Ideally, in club meetings, in letters to the editor, and in demands for equal time on rightist radio stations, we should all speak out against extremism. These efforts would not stave off the re-emergence of the far Right, but they might dilute

[43] Westin, "The Deadly Parallels," p. 32.

some of its influence. In some areas of the state the dangers of speaking out include loss of job, dead cats tossed on the porch, harassment of speakers at community forums, and anonymous phone calls in the middle of the night. Demanding radio rebuttal carries unique dangers. If church leaders, for example, are Communist-dominated, who would step forward and qualify as the offended party wanting equal time? Paying the price of such dangers is not always worth it in individual instances. But unless the nonextremists publicize their views, the far Right will have an easier time in reasserting its influence.

The public schools, a particular target of Texas extremists, must be zealously watched over by all who favor scholarship and a genuine search for truth. Citizens have a right and a duty to criticize their schools. They also have a right to expect a clear assessment of what is involved in censorship from the mass media, publishers, teachers, and community leaders. Only the weekly *Texas Observer* provided its readers with detailed coverage of the censorship fights. When the D. C. Heath Company sent letters to dozens of publishers suggesting that they work together to combat the criticism in Texas, only a few publishers approved. And since the jobs of teachers and town leaders depend in part on avoiding controversial issues, little hope of speaking out is offered from these quarters either. Yet the ultimate answer to the censorship problem depends upon public insistence that scholars, and not pressure groups, decide what is to be in a textbook.

Unfortunately, a public insistence upon scholarship is not apt to arrive until Texas outgrows its historical background of anti-intellectualism—the Establishment's hegemony of business and rural primitivism. As Rice University biology professor Clark Read noted:

Education is only just now coming into its own as an important factor in social mobility in the Southwest. During the late 19th century and up into the present, business criteria . . . have dominated Southwestern culture almost without challenge. In our section of the country these criteria contained a curious mixture of values derived from the petroleum industry, ranching, and Judge Roy Bean. It was long assumed that schooling existed for the single purpose of making personal advancement possible. Intellectual and cultural pursuits have been considered unmanly, unworldly, and certainly impractical. . . .

In Texas, the relationship between business and university faculties is very much like that between the Romans and their Greek slaves. In ancient Rome the slaves were the teachers of the children of the Romans. However, we must point out that during this period the Greeks made no new contributions to knowledge. They simply taught what had been learned before. This is essentially what has been going on in Texas institutions, with the fairly important additional consideration that on many of the campuses of Texas the faculty have not been allowed to keep up with what is going on. They can only truly keep up with what went on before they entered the faculty of the institution. In Texas we suffer from an outsized materialistic barbarism. The businessman in Texas has not been a civilized man nor a civilized agent of man.[44]

The rightist outbursts seem cumulatively to whittle away liberties. Each one seems to accustom us to lack of freedom, making it harder to resist the next attack, especially when it is clothed in the name of national security. A community is dissolving when everyone eyes his neighbor as a possible enemy, when religious and political nonconformity are marks of disaffection, and when mere denunciation takes the place of evidence. Such fears may eventually subject us to a despotism as evil as any that we dread.

We must not stifle dissent, of course, whether from the Right or the Left. But if there is to be any abridgment of the First Amendment, it ought not to apply only to the extreme Left. In 1951 the Supreme Court upheld the Smith Act, which invaded the free speech of Communists, who were simply talking about revolution. Since 1961 this approach has been softened by the Court's holding that the Smith Act covers only "active" members of the Communist party. If it must cover active Communists, it should also apply to active Birchers and fascists, who are every bit as revolutionary as the Communists. An even better approach might be to repeal the Smith Act. Ultimate futility of attempts to compel obedience is the lesson of every effort from the Roman drive to stamp

[44] Clark Read, column in the *Texas Observer*, June 11, 1965.

out Christianity as a disturber of pagan unity, the Inquisition as a means to religious and dynastic unity, Siberian exile as a tool of Russian unity, down to the mass murders of the Nazis.

We must not stifle dissent, but we must counteract the propaganda of the right-wing extremists. It is they, more than any other single political or ethnic group, who hope to destroy the first and fifth amendments, who enjoy preying upon racial hatreds, and who try to suppress the public schools' curricula. John F. Kennedy was due in Austin on November 22, 1963, and he planned to say: "This country is moving and it must not stop. It cannot stop. This is a time for courage and a time for challenge. Neither conformity nor complacency will do. Neither the fanatics nor the faint-hearted are needed."[45]

[45] *Texas Observer*, December 27, 1963.

# Huey Long and the Politics of Realism

T. HARRY WILLIAMS

IN JANUARY, 1934, Senator Tom Connally of Texas presented a report to his colleagues of the upper chamber that left them in a state of confusion. Connally was the chairman of a special committee on campaign expenditures, and now he was summarizing the result of a lengthy inquiry into a Senate election in Louisiana. In the election of 1932 the incumbent senator, Edwin Broussard, had been defeated by John H. Overton. But Broussard and his supporters had immediately charged that the election was void because fraud had been used to achieve Overton's victory. Broussard had not claimed that he had been elected, but he had insisted that Overton should not be allowed to take his seat and that a new election should be called. He had asked the Senate to prove the fraud by sending its special committee on campaign expenses to Louisiana to conduct an investigation. It would take a Senate committee to uncover the evidence, Broussard said, because the fraud had been devised and directed by the boss of the state, Overton's principal backer, that master of crooked politics, Senator Huey P. Long.

The committee had begun its investigation late in 1932, had resumed it early in 1933, and had concluded it in the last months of that year. In the meantime Overton had been permitted to take his seat, but his right to it was under a cloud. If the special committee should decide that he had been fraudulently elected, the Senate might well expel him. Hence when chairman Connally rose to give his report, his associates listened eagerly. But when he had finished, the Senators could not make out what he was recommending. He stated that devices conducive to fraud had been used in Overton's behalf and that fraud probably had occurred in the election. But he also said that the committee had not been able to establish that the fraud had influenced the outcome of the election or that Overton had been aware of it. The Senate, naturally puzzled as to what course to take, referred the report to the committee on elections. This agency advised that as there was insufficient evidence to show that Overton had been elected fraudulently, he was entitled to retain his seat. Connally reluctantly concurred in the decision. He had had some unpleasant experiences during the investigation, and he declared bitterly, "I advise anyone who thinks he knows something about politics to go down in Louisiana and take a postgraduate course."[1]

[1] *Congressional Record*, 73rd Cong., 2d sess., 1934, 1552–64. The sources for some of the statements in this paper are persons I interviewed while doing research on a biography of Huey P. Long. Since

Connally was himself something of an expert on politics, a graduate of the Texas school of the art, which has produced some notable students. But even with this background, he was appalled by some quality in Louisiana politics, something different and somehow evil. He publicly condemned this quality, but perhaps secretly or unconsciously he admired it. Other observers have also noted this element of difference and have attributed it to the professionalism that has always characterized the state's politics. That perceptive critic of our own time, A. J. Liebling, wrote, "Louisiana politics is of an intensity and complexity that are matched, in my experience, only in the Republic of Lebanon." Liebling concluded that the state as a whole, but especially its southern section, was a part of the Hellenistic-Mediterranean littoral. Its psychology, he said, was sensual, speculative, devious; in a flash of inspiration he named Louisiana the "westernmost of the Arab states."[2]

No such sociological analysis had occurred to Connally. He had a ready explanation to account for the uniqueness of Louisiana: the state was what it was because it was ruled by a bad and corrupt man, Huey Long. But behind the simplistic explanation were factors of which Connally was doubtless unaware. He detested Huey personally, considering the Kingfish to be crude and domineering, a man who did not belong

---

some of these individuals prefer to remain anonymous, I have not cited the names of any interviewees in the notes.

[2] A. J. Liebling, "The Great State," *New Yorker*, May 28, 1960, p. 48, and June 11, 1960, p. 100.

in the company of gentlemen. More important, he hated and feared Long's political ideas, viewing them as radical, probably un-American and definitely un-Southern.

Connally's opinion was shared by nearly all other Southern senators. Huey Long of Louisiana had almost no friends among the Southerners in the Senate. His closest associates were men from Northern or Western states, progressive Democrats, and, significantly, progressive Republicans: Burton K. Wheeler, George W. Norris, William E. Borah, and Bronson Cutting. Long, for his part, had little use for most of the Southern senators and representatives. He judged them to be no different from most Republicans, conservatives who were blind to the signs of the time, men who did not practice a politics of realism.

Connally was right, however, in one section of his evaluation; he did not exaggerate the power of Huey Long in Louisiana. After becoming governor in 1928, Long gradually erected a power structure unique in the record of American politics, the most daring and dangerous concentration of power ever created in an American state. Unlike other Southern mass leaders—mass leader is a more accurate term than demagogue to characterize leaders like Long—he did not permit his program to be sabotaged by the conservative opposition. He set himself not just to contain this opposition, but to overwhelm and finally destroy it.

He had almost achieved his goal by 1934 and did reach it

the following year, when he forced the last remaining strong opposition faction to come into his organization on his terms. Then he stood almost supreme. Controlling the political structure of the state, he controlled also its government, all three branches of it. A compliant Longite governor, elected in 1932 after Long went to the Senate, headed the executive branch, a Longite majority of more than two-thirds dominated the legislature, and Longite judges outnumbered anti-Long judges on the supreme court.

The magnitude of this power structure evoked admiration even from some of his enemies, who, being Louisianians and hence instinctive politicians, appreciated his achievement while resenting its effect. I asked a leader of the Old Regular faction in New Orleans, the powerful city machine that fought Long but was finally broken by him, to explain the reason for Huey's success. This man had disliked Huey personally and opposed his ideas, but had eventually gone over to him. His reply was almost venerative: "Others had power in their organization, but he had power in himself. And he brought them all to their knees."

The bases of Long's power were several. He had a superb organization, and he was a leader endowed with the mysterious quality we call charism, which indeed gave him power in himself. But organization and charism do not quite explain the hold he secured and retained on the masses of Louisiana. The secret of his power, in the final analysis, was in his pro-

gram—he promised something to the people and delivered it.
He gave them things they had long yearned for and thought
they would never get, and this they could not forget. "They do
not merely vote for him, they worship the ground he walks
on," a puzzled Northern reporter wrote. "He is a part of
their religion."[3]

His program may not seem very far-reaching by today's
standards—a modern road system, the improvement and
humanizing of facilities in state hospitals and other institutions, increased appropriations for education and free textbooks for all school children, the beginnings of a public health
service, free night schools for adult illiterates, a homestead
exemption law that lightened the taxes, particularly of poor
people, and abolition of the poll tax that prevented many poor
people from voting. But by the standards of the time, and
especially in a Southern state, it was a liberal, if not a radical,
program. Every item in it, incidentally, could have been provided by the state's previous rulers if they had had any sense
of social responsibility.

It is not my purpose here to attempt a general evaluation of
Huey Long. I have elsewhere denied the accuracy of a label
often applied to him, that he was a demagogue.[4] The term has

---

[3] Paul Anderson, *St. Louis Post-Dispatch*, March 3, 1935.

[4] T. Harry Williams, "The Gentleman from Louisiana: Demagogue or Democrat," *Journal of Southern History*, 26 (February,
1960), 3–21; idem, *Romance and Realism in Southern Politics*
(Athens: University of George Press, 1961), pp. 65–84.

been fixed on other American politicians, sometimes by their enemies and sometimes by scholars, but, regardless of who does the fixing, it is seldom invested with any precise definition. The term was coined by the Greeks and for them it had meaning. The demagogue was a man of "loose tongue . . . trusting to tumult" who led "the populace to mischief with empty words." He was, it should be noted, a man who operated in a small city-state and who could lead a mob to force the portals of power.

The term obviously has little validity for a modern country like the United States, yet we continue to use it. We mean by it, if anything, a leader who arouses people by promises he does not mean to keep. Long, who was a remarkably introspective politician, devoted much thought to whether he deserved the title of demagogue. He concluded, and rightly it seems to me, that he did not, for he had not deceived the people but had kept his promise to them.

I have denied too the accuracy of another label pinned on Long, that he was a dictator, the first great American fascist. The dictator label is also of European origin and, in my opinion, has little, if any, meaning when applied to the American scene. An American leader or boss may achieve great power, but he cannot retain it indefinitely. He has at periodic intervals to return to the people to ask for a renewal of power; they at any time are likely to repudiate him. This is a truth that, interestingly, Long realized. He knew that his power structure was a temporary thing, to be operated only by him. He re-

peatedly warned his associates, or possible heirs, not to attempt to use his powers, for if they did they would come to
tragic ends.

If Long was not a dictator, then what was he? It could be
argued that he was an extension of the boss type, unusually
imaginative and daring, but still just a boss. But the boss label
does not quite describe him. He went beyond other bosses in
his genius for devising power, in his readiness to use it, and
in his delight at possessing it. He differed from the boss type
also in his capacity to stand off and view himself, measure his
actions, and plan his future. He mapped out his political
career before he attained his majority: he would first win a
secondary state office, then he would be governor, next he
would be a senator, and finally he would be president. This
forecasting might be dismissed as the dream of a bumptious
youth if he had not executed the first three parts of it and if
before his death he had not seemed about to fulfill it completely. He had a sense of destiny unusual in a politician or a
boss.

The most revealing term to apply to him is one suggested
by Eric Hoffer to describe the man who shakes the existing
order and gives a new direction to history—mass leader. The
mass leader appears when conditions demand change. Thus he
is a product of or a response to existing conditions, but he
may determine that change, which has to come, will take a
certain direction, even a revolutionary direction. He builds a
mass movement out of the frustrations of man. He harnesses

man's hungers and fears to a holy cause and drives or leads men to a great end. He must have certain qualities: audacity, an iron will, faith in himself and his cause, brazenness, and an ability to arouse a sense of collectivity among his followers. He may lead men to freedom and plenty, or he may enslave them.[5]

Huey Long had all the qualities of a mass leader. Because he had them, he was able to overcome his opposition in Louisiana, to enact his program of social reform, to build his great power structure. But his ambitions did not stop with Louisiana; they soared to national levels. He intended to become president, and after he became senator, he put forward a program that he believed would take him to the highest office. He called it Share Our Wealth, and it sounded a new and different note in Southern and even in American politics. It was, as Long admitted, a radical program. Indeed, he said that both he and the program were of "the left," being, to my knowledge, the only politician of a major party who has dared to adopt the leftist label. He frequently declared that if America was to go forward, she would have to go left.

It was a program designed to make him president, but it was also a program in which he believed, one that he wanted to have made a reality regardless of whether he became president. As I read him, he had a genuine concern for poor people.

[5] Eric Hoffer, *The True Believer: Thoughts on the Nature of Mass Movements* (New York: Harper and Brothers, Publishers, 1951), passim.

He wanted to lift these people up, in his state, in his region, and in the nation. He once said in the Senate, in perhaps his most eloquent address to that body: "Nonetheless, my voice will be the same as it has been. Patronage will not change it. Fear will not change it. Persecution will not change it. It cannot be changed while people suffer. The only way it can be changed is to make the lives of these people decent and respectable."[6]

Long unveiled his Share Our Wealth program in a radio address over a national hookup on the night of February 23, 1934. The fight to decentralize wealth had entered a new phase, he told his listeners: it had achieved the advantage of organization. The organization had been created by people whom he identified only as "we" (he should have said "me"); it had a name, the Share Our Wealth Society, and a slogan, "Every Man a King." He exhorted his hearers to join the society, to get together in their communities and form local chapters. If they needed instructions on how to proceed, they should write him. He emphasized that in the society there would be no national dues.

He also outlined the principles of the society. These were not entirely new. He had expounded them in Senate speeches since he had arrived in that body in January, 1932, and he had discussed them as governor of Louisiana and even earlier when

6 *American Progress*, April, 1935.

he was chairman of the state Public Service Commission. He had, in fact, been talking about them since he had been a high school youth in his home town of Winnfield. They were an outgrowth of the neo-Populist background in which he grew up, modified later as a result of his observation of the economy and his reading about it. They were his answer to what he believed to be a crisis in American capitalism—the growing concentration of wealth, a development the New Deal was doing nothing to halt. Wealth had to be redistributed, he said, or capitalism would fall before a communist revolution. Always before he had spoken of "redistribution" of wealth. But now he substituted the more catchy "share."

The basic plank in the plan was a limitation on wealth. The national government would impose a capital levy that would prevent a family from owning a fortune of more than $5 million or more than three hundred times the fortune of the average American family. The government would impose an income tax that would prohibit a family from earning more than $1 million a year, or more than three hundred times the income of the average family. Just as there would be a ceiling on wealth, there would be a floor under poverty. From the revenue derived from its taxes, the government would provide every family in the country with a "homestead" of $5,000, or "enough for a home, an automobile, a radio, and the ordinary conveniences." The government would further guarantee that every family would receive an annual income of $2,000 to $3,000, or one-third of the average family income.

Other benefits would be furnished by the government. It would give pensions of $30 a month to the aged (this figure was later eliminated and the word "adequate" substituted), finance the college education of boys and girls of demonstrated ability (later Long would advocate that the federal government and the states should jointly bear the costs of educating also students below the college level), and pay generous bonuses to veterans. Moreover, the government would limit the hours of labor to thirty hours a week and eleven months a year, thus increasing the need for workers. And because Long thought it was senseless to destroy food while people went hungry, the government would purchase and store agricultural surpluses, thus balancing farm supply with demand.[7]

Huey's announcement of Share Our Wealth set off an extended public discussion as to the nature of his plan. Was SOW a radical formula, or did it only seem radical? Was it compatible with capitalism, or would it transform the American system into something quite different? Some critics denounced the plan as a form of socialism, charging that the rate of taxation would eventually eliminate all fortunes and reduce all incomes to approximately the same level. Huey heatedly denied the socialism charge. The Socialists, he said, advocated government ownership of wealth, which was equivalent to destruction of wealth. His plan would retain the profit motive and, by preventing the concentration of wealth, would

7 *Congressional Record*, 73rd Cong., 2d Sess., 1934, 3450–53.

remove the worst abuse in the capitalistic system and really strengthen it. In fact, because the plan would prevent a few men from controlling the wealth of the country, more, not fewer, millionaires would be created. Once a leftist interviewer suggested to Huey that he then proposed to save the very magnates he denounced. "That would be one of the unfortunate effects of my plan," the Kingfish genially admitted. "I'd cut their nails and file their teeth and let them live."[8]

Other critics contended that SOW was unsound economically. They declared that Long conceived of wealth only in terms of money and overlooked the importance of the machinery that produced wealth. His plan might spread money, the symbol of wealth, around, but it would not increase the amount of wealth. Some of the critics doubted that the plan would even spread existing wealth very much. How, for example, they asked, would Huey proceed with an organization like the Ford Motor Company? How could he make a factory that produced cars produce houses? The government could tax Ford's profits, but the resulting revenue would provide only a small part of the benefits that Huey had promised. And if the government taxed both the company's income and assets at the rate proposed by SOW, it would end up owning most of the stock of the company, and then Mr. Ford would tell the government to run the business itself.

Huey attempted to answer the criticisms of the economic

[8] Rose Lee, "Senator Long at Home," *New Republic*, 79 (May 30, 1934), 68.

features of his plan. He explained that wealth would not necessarily be distributed in the form of money. It could be passed around in the form of goods. Thus a man who needed a house or a car could be given one from the possessions of a man who had too many of them for his own use. Or, a poor man could be given a block of stock that had come into the hands of the government through taxation. He admitted, however, that some details of his plan remained to be worked on. "I am going to have to call in some great minds to help me," he said.[9]

His plan might have faults, but it was not the visionary thing his critics painted it to be. When they said that it would not increase wealth, they were saying, to use a more modern phrasing, that it would not cause economic growth. This was manifestly wrong. Any program of large and sustained expenditure by government will result in an expanded economy, as we know from the experience of our own time. Huey's principal omission was that he did not provide for continued financing. His capital levy would have been largely a one-shot source of income. That is, the revenue from it would have decreased dramatically after the first year, and to keep the program of benefits going the government would have had to resort to deficit financing. With his quick mind, he would undoubtedly have soon grasped this necessity, the device that modern government uses to sustain the economy. The problem of modern government is not to foster growth but to ensure

[9] *New York Times*, March 9, 1935.

that the resulting wealth is evenly distributed. Huey, with his guaranteed "homestead" and guaranteed national income, went beyond anything yet done by government to keep wealth distributed.

Huey produced his plan during the depression, a time that tempted plans. Other men dreamed of ways to combat the economic ills afflicting the nation and proposed their schemes. Father Coughlin, the radio priest, assured his millions of listeners that the single expedient of inflating the currency with silver would end the depression. Dr. Francis Townsend enlisted a huge following with his proposal to increase mass purchasing power: he would give all elderly people generous monthly pensions that would have to be spent each month. Novelist Upton Sinclair, turning his talents to politics, attracted national attention with a plan to end poverty by having the government buy or lease land, on which the jobless could raise their own food, and rent idle factories, in which the unemployed could produce their own clothes and other necessities.

Huey's plan differed from the others in being more complex and far-reaching. The plans of Coughlin, Townsend, and Sinclair were essentially formulas for recovery only. They might have lifted the country out of the depression, but they would not have changed significantly the existing economic structure or existing economic relationships. Huey's plan was also designed to hasten recovery, but, in addition, it would have altered meaningfully the power relations of the economy.

The national government would have assumed a larger and a permanent role in directing the economic system.

Share Our Wealth was not a hasty formula cooked up to make political capital, and its author's interest in economics was not just an aberration of the moment. Huey Long had been interested in economic questions since his first campaign. It was this emphasis that set him apart from other Southern politicians of his time. In an age when Southern aspirants for office either entertained their audiences of rural poor with tales of how their grandpappies had won glory in the Civil War or excited the passions of these audiences with denunciations of Reconstruction and Yankees and "niggers," Long discussed economic issues of the present, issues that mattered. He asked the South to turn its gaze from the past to the present and to do something itself about its problems. It was this departure from the pattern that caused commentator Gerald Johnson to say that Long was the first Southerner since the great Virginians of the eighteenth century to extend the boundaries of political thought. Long's emphasis on economics was part of his politics of realism.[10]

He departed again from the Southern pattern in his attitude toward Negroes. In his time in Louisiana they were not restive in their situation, or, if they were, they did not voice their feelings or demand a change in their status. They were similar-

[10] Gerald W. Johnson, "Live Demagogue, or Dead Gentleman?" *Virginia Quarterly Review*, 12 (Winter, 1936), 9–11.

ly quiet throughout most of the South, and the politicians ignored them—except during campaigns, when some votes could always be picked up by denouncing the "nigger danger." Huey could have ignored them too, but he did not.

Huey had rarely exploited the racial issue in his campaigns on his rise to power, and when he did use it he did not do it very skillfully, being obviously uncomfortable with the subject. But after he became governor and senator, he discussed the racial problem on frequent occasions. In these pronouncements he seemed to be a typical white Southerner—he was for segregation and white supremacy all the way. He repeatedly stated that he favored leaving the question of whether Negroes should vote to the respective states (which of course would enable the South to continue disfranchising them), and as senator he consistently opposed a federal antilynching law as unnecessary and an invasion of States' rights.

His talk, his whole racial stance was, however, a strategy. By seeming to be a complete segregationist, he reserved for himself a freedom of action on racial matters. He could then do some things that breached the pattern of segregation; he could give the Negroes certain rights that he believed they should have. The rights that he would extend were economic ones. He felt a genuine sympathy for the material plight of the blacks. "Now, just a word about the poor Negroes," he said while he was governor. "They're here. They've got to be cared for. The poor Negroes have to live too." He was never very explicit in defining the economic rights the Negroes should have, probably because he thought these rights were so apparent they did not have to be listed. When a reporter asked him in 1935 how he would treat Negroes when he became president, he answered, "Treat them just the same as everybody else, give them an opportunity to make a living." He added that Negroes should have "a chance to work and make a living, and to get an education."[11]

The Negroes in Louisiana shared in the benefits of the Long program: the free schoolbooks, the free facilities at the state hospitals, the public health services. Indeed, because they were poorer than the poorest whites, they benefited more from the program. Thus the homestead exemption law exempted 77 percent of the homes of white people from taxation but 95 percent of the homes of black people. Huey realized the racial implications of his program. As one of his leaders explained his reasoning: "You can't help poor white people without helping poor Negroes. It has to be that way."

The privileges that Huey wanted to extend to Negroes may seem small to today's generation, but for his time they were large, more than other Southern politicians were willing to grant. At the same time there was a limit to what he would do. He would carry the Negroes only as far as he safely could at the moment. He would raise their economic and educational standards—because he could accomplish that. He would not attempt to extend the suffrage to them—because if he did, he

[11] *Louisiana Progress*, August 18, 1931; *Boston Daily Evening Transcript*, January 11, 1935; *Baton Rouge State Times*, June 3, 1935.

would fail and would fail in everything else he wanted to do. He once tried to explain his dilemma to a Negro interviewer. "I have been able to do a hell of a lot of things down there because I am Huey Long," he said. "A lot of guys would have been murdered politically for what I've been able to do quietly for niggers."

He also tried to put over to this interviewer that in a Southern state it was difficult to do things for Negroes. A politician had to resort to stratagems to accomplish justice. As an example, he related what he had had to do to persuade whites that blacks should share equally in the public health facilities maintained by Louisiana. "I said to them, 'You wouldn't want a colored woman watching over your children if she had pyorrhea, would you?' They see the point."[12]

What he did do earned him the deep gratitude of Negroes, especially of those in the South. The Negro press of the region was unanimous in praising him. Although these papers noted that he had helped Negroes with his program, they expressed their greatest appreciation for his refusal to indulge in "nigger baiting." Unlike his predecessors in Louisiana, "He has not ridden to power on the 'Negro question,' " one editor said.[13]

More revealing of Negro opinion, and moving in their simple eloquence, are the statements of Negroes who were young

[12] Roy Wilkins, "Huey Long Says—An Interview with the Louisiana Kingfish," *Crisis*, 42 (February, 1935), 41, 52.
[13] *Nashville Globe*, June 7, 1935.

persons in Huey's time and who, although they live in an era when their people enjoy greater rights than he dreamed of, yet think of him as one who prepared the way for that era. The consensus of their statements is that he opened the door—not very wide perhaps, but he opened it—and, what bulks large with them, he opened it although he could have kept it shut, being one of the very few white leaders to act without pressure. Some examples of their remarks follow. A man who acted as a chauffeur for state officials: "There was not a finer man. Nothing wrong with him. He always treated me fine." A laborer: "He was fair to colored people, good to all poor people. He walked the land like Jesus Christ and left nothing undone." A schoolteacher: "We felt that he had no prejudices. He gave the Negroes and all poor people hope."

Long was determined to establish his politics of realism on the national level. He had completed his plans to achieve his goal in 1935, the year that he met his death by assassination. In the presidential election of 1936 he would run a third-party candidate, some ranking progressive Democrat or Republican, against Franklin D. Roosevelt in the hope of taking enough votes to throw the election to the Republicans. The Republicans, he thought, would be incapable of dealing with the depression, the economic system would collapse, and by 1940 the country would be crying for a strong man to rescue it. Then Huey Long would be elected president and would take over and put the pieces together as—as he wanted to put them.

But how would he put them together? Was he going to use the frustrations of men as mortar to build a brave new and theoretical world of his dreams? Would he stop short of enslaving men to save them? It was to help people that he had seized power and then more power, until he had become obsessed with the conviction that he could not do what he had to do without reaching for yet more power. Would he ever have enough power? He could not tell, himself.